D0530384

ADRIAN WALLWORK

BUSINESS
OPTIONS
WORKBOOK

OXFORD
UNIVERSITY PRESS

Oxford University Press,
Great Clarendon Street, Oxford OX2 6DP

Oxford New York
Athens Auckland Bangkok Bogotá
Buenos Aires Calcutta Cape Town Chennai
Dar es Salaam Delhi Florence Hong Kong
Istanbul Karachi Kuala Lumpur Madrid
Melbourne Mexico City Mumbai Nairobi
Paris São Paulo Singapore Taipei Tokyo
Toronto Warsaw

and associated companies in
Berlin Ibadan

OXFORD and OXFORD ENGLISH
are trade marks of Oxford University Press

ISBN 0 19 457236 6

Printed in China

Acknowledgements

Illustrations by:
Ned Jolliffe p 54
Nigel Paige pp 5, 8, 21, 24, 25, 37, 42, 46, 49, 51, 53, 66
Technical Graphics Department, Oxford University Press pp 15,
26, 31, 39, 55

The publishers would like to thank the following for the
permission to reproduce photographs:

Image Bank pp 41, 61
Karrass Ltd., Santa Monica p 62
Orion Press, Tokyo p 40
Rex Features p 28
Tony Stone Images pp 7, 19, 23, 50, 59
Whirlpool PLC p 58

Commissioned photography by:
Barker Evans Photography pp 30, 45

Design: Sarah Nicholson

The authors and publisher are grateful to those who have given
permission to reproduce the following extracts and adaptations
of copyright material:

p 5 *The Xenophobe's Guide to the English* by Antony Miall,
published by Ravette Books Limited. Copyright © Oval Projects
Ltd. 1993.
p 12 *Introduction to Management* by Richard Pettinger © Richard
Pettinger 1994. Reproduced by permission of Macmillan Press
Ltd.
p 19 *Practical NLP for Managers* by Ian McDermott and Joseph
O'Connor © Ian McDermott and Joseph O'Connor 1996.
Reprinted by permission of Gower Publishing Limited.
p 27 *Your Personality Quiz Book* by Dr Glenn Wilson. Copyright ©
1994 Glenn Wilson. Reproduced by permission of publisher
Hodder and Stoughton.
p 28 *Do's and Taboos of Preparing for your Trip Abroad* by Roger
Axtell and John Healy. Copyright © 1994 by Roger E. Axtell and
John P. Healy. Reprinted by permission of John Wiley & Sons, Inc.
p 33 Excerpts from *Principles of Economics*, copyright © 1998 by
N. Gregory Mankiw, reprinted by permission of Harcourt Brace &
Company.
p 43 'The American Way' from *A Guide to Doing Business in the
USA*. Copyright © 1991 Sun Microsystems, Inc. All rights reserved.
Reprinted with permission.
p 50 *Presentations Plus* by David Peoples. Copyright © 1992 by
David A. Peoples. Reprinted by permission of John Wiley & Sons,
Inc.
p 58 'Restructured Whirlpool Advances 58%' by Nikki Tait,
appeared in the *Financial Times* 21 April 1998. Reprinted by
permission of the *Financial Times*.
p 62 *Negotiate to Close* by Gary Karrass.

Although every effort has been made to trace and contact
copyright holders before publication, this has not always been
possible. We apologize for any apparent infringement of
copyright and if notified, the publisher will be pleased to rectify
any errors or omissions at the earliest opportunity.

Contents

1 PROTOCOL

1 Introductions   Write replies to the following.

1   Hey, how are you doing? ....

2   Good to see you again. ....

3   Pleased to meet you. ....

4   My name's Tomas Bartha. ....

5   I've heard a lot about you. ....

6   Beautiful weather, isn't it? ....

7   Sorry, I've forgotten your name. ....

8   Well, it's been great seeing you again. ....

9   Say 'hello' to Olaf Bouwermeister for me. ....

10   See you tomorrow. ....

2 Question forms   **1** The questions below have all been asked at job interviews in the UK. Put the verbs in brackets into the correct form. Then circle the numbers of those questions that you believe it is not legitimate to ask at job interviews.

1   (You think) .... of having any children in the near future?

2   Tell me about the best manager (you ever have) .... The worst?

3   (You have) .... a happy childhood?

4   (You have) .... to work long hours in your last job? How (you feel) .... about this?

5   (You ever convict) .... of a criminal offence?

6   How much (you drink) .... ? Smoke? How often? Why?

7   What (you consider) .... to be your strongest qualities? What are your weaknesses and what (you do) .... about them?

8   What (you generally do) .... in the evenings? At weekends? On holiday?

9   What (you see yourself) .... doing in five years' time? And ten?

10   What ('success' mean) .... to you?

2 Now, briefly answer any five questions.

....

....

....

....

....

3 Job description

Your company wishes to take part in an international project with three or four other countries. As part of their bid to get funding for the project, your company has been asked to supply a brief resume of the project leaders. Your boss has asked you to write such a resume for yourself. Write a resume of around 200 words.

4 The English

Read these extracts from a book entitled 'Xenophobe's guide to the English', which takes a satirical look at the English. Match each extract with one of these titles:

A How others see them **C** How they would like to be seen
B How they see themselves

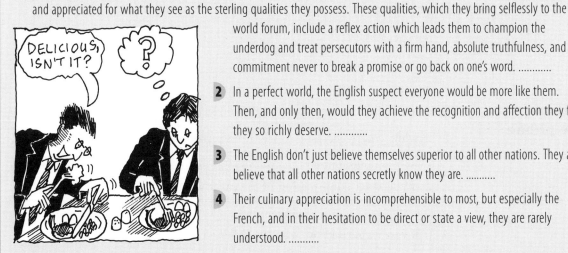

1 Although it is impossible for the English to appear to care what others think of them, deep down they would like to be loved and appreciated for what they see as the sterling qualities they possess. These qualities, which they bring selflessly to the world forum, include a reflex action which leads them to champion the underdog and treat persecutors with a firm hand, absolute truthfulness, and a commitment never to break a promise or go back on one's word. ....

2 In a perfect world, the English suspect everyone would be more like them. Then, and only then, would they achieve the recognition and affection they feel they so richly deserve. ....

3 The English don't just believe themselves superior to all other nations. They also believe that all other nations secretly know they are. ....

4 Their culinary appreciation is incomprehensible to most, but especially the French, and in their hesitation to be direct or state a view, they are rarely understood. ....

5 To outsiders the English are intellectually impenetrable. They express little emotion. They are not so much slow as stationary to anger and the pleasures of life seem to pass them by as they revel in discomfort and self-denial. ....

6 With an unparalleled sense of historical continuity, they appear to carry on in their own sweet way largely unmoved by developments in the world around them. ....

7 With their wealth of experience of 'running the show' as they see it, they are also deeply aware of their responsibilities to others. They see it as their solemn duty to protect the weak, strengthen the faint-hearted and shame bullies into submission. ....

5 Test your protocol

Mark the following statements true (*T*) or false (*F*).

1 In Japan, you should pass your business card with your right hand. ☐

2 It is uncommon for people in the Far East to use the word 'no'. ☐

3 Mrs Tau Pei Lin, a Chinese lady, asks you to call her by her first name. You should ☐ call her 'Tau'.

4 In Europe, when kissing someone on an informal occasion you should give the person the following number of kisses:

a Netherlands: 3 ☐   **b** Italy: 2 ☐   **c** Britain: 1 ☐   **d** France: 4 ☐   **e** Russia: 3 ☐

5 Men in Russia often walk arm in arm. ☐

6 The floor at ground level in the USA is called the first floor not the ground floor. ☐

7 Canadians don't mind being referred to as Americans. ☐

8 Wales is part of England. ☐

9 Making a circle with your thumb and forefinger, with the other fingers pointing up, ☐ is an international sign meaning 'OK'.

10 Looking people straight in the eye (for a few seconds) is acceptable in all cultures. ☐

6 Answering the phone

When you answer the phone, what do you say …

1 …while you're checking to see if the person wanted is in the office?

....

2 …if you want confirmation of the caller's name?

....

3 …if you want to know who the caller is?

....

4 …if the caller has had to wait a long time to be connected?

....

5 …if you didn't understand what the caller said?

....

6 …if the caller is speaking too fast?

....

7 ...if the line is bad?

....

8 ...if the person wanted is in a meeting?

....

9 ...if you want to check you've taken down the right number?

....

10 ...before you put the phone down?

....

7 Telephone dialogue

Underline the correct forms in *italics*, and complete the missing spaces with appropriate phrases. Note that some are questions and some are statements.

A Metafora Informatica. Buon giorno.

B *I am / This is* [1] David Friedmann from Solomon's in London.

....[2] Mr Rossi please?

A ....[3] Mr Rossi *there isn't / isn't here* [4]. He's at lunch.

B Well, ...[5] *me back / back me* [6] please?

A Could you ....[7]?

B Yes it's F-R-I-E-D-M-A-double N.

A Double N?

B Yes, ...[8]. And my number is 0044–171–3246123.

A I'm sorry, ...[9]? The line is really bad.

B Yes, of course. It's 0044–171–3246123.

A So that's David Friedmann on 0044–171–3246123.

B ....[10].

A OK Mr Friedmann, ...[11].

B Thank you very much. Goodbye.

A Goodbye.

2 MEETINGS

1 Call a meeting

Some people have strong feelings about meetings. How do you think the writer of this poster feels?

**Lonely? Looking for company? Having trouble passing the time?
Find decision-making difficult?**

Why not have a meeting!

Meetings are the way to meet people, catch up on your sleep, avoid making decisions, feel important, and impress your colleagues.

And all in work time!

Meetings

The practical alternative to work.

2 The ideal meeting?

Look at this advice about participating in meetings, and match the beginning of each point with its ending. Do you notice anything strange?

1 Announce the meeting five minutes before it is scheduled to take place; *b*

2 Do not take time to check the agenda beforehand; *f*

3 If you are chairing the meeting, start off with a long introduction; *a*

4 Feel free to leave the meeting ... *c*

5 If you are not officially involved in the meeting ... *d*

6 Whatever you do, do not publish the minutes of the meeting ... *e*

a this will make you feel important, and the attendees will be reassured that no real decisions will be made.

b this creates a sense of urgency and ensures that no one can prepare for the meeting.

c if you have a more important problem to deal with elsewhere.

d feel free to join in, appear interested, and ask a couple of questions before walking out.

e until the next one has taken place.

f though it would be even better not to have an agenda at all.

3 Word stress

Below are three columns of words with three syllables. Mark the words that do not correspond to the stress pattern of the first word in the column, and indicate which column they should be in, as in the examples.

1	2	3
agency Ooo	investment oOo	engineer ooO
effective ...2...	*calculate* ...1...	*organize* ...1...
agenda	agreement	consumer ....
deficit	approval	committee ....
industry	assignment	employee ....
integrate	character	guarantee ....
marketing	commercial	override ....
objective	database	personal ....
proceedings	enquiry	personnel ....
salary	management	register ....
strategy	procedure	represent ....
turnover	projection	revenue ....

4 Useful phrases: politics

Combine a word from the box on the left with one on the right to produce a new word or phrase, then match it to its meaning.

band	old	smear
swing	dark	exit
fund	grass	land

campaign	guard	vote
wagon	raiser	horse
slide	roots	poll

1 political party or movement that readily attracts supporters because of its mass appeal or apparent strength ....

2 veteran political figures, often resistant to new ideas ....

3 determining vote in close election, often one that changes at the last moment ....

4 crude, unsubstantiated attacks against opposing candidate ....

5 relative unknown, underdog in election ....

6 overwhelming majority of votes ....

7 event held to raise money for candidate or cause ....

8 ordinary voters, the rank and file of a constituency ....

9 survey to assess preferences immediately after voting ....

5 More political terms

Complete the crossword, using the clues below. The clues refer to the British political system; can you use the same terms in yours?

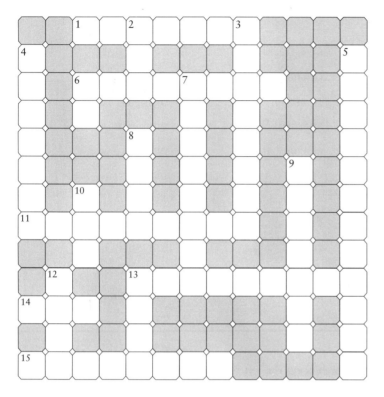

Across

1   Committee of senior government ministers. (noun)

6   Head of a government department. (noun)

11   .... of State: a minister who heads a major government department. (noun)

13   Reorganization of ministries; usually once per year in the UK. (noun; can also be a verb)

14   Help, particularly to developing countries or when natural disasters have occurred. (noun; can also be a verb)

15   Process of choosing representatives by popular vote. (noun)

Down

2   Forbid. (verb; can also be a noun)

3   Government department which controls public finances. (noun)

4   The UK Parliament is divided into the House of Lords and the House of .... (noun)

5   A geographically-defined district with its own elected representative. (noun)

6   Member of Parliament. (abbreviation)

7   Actions which cause public feelings of outrage. (noun, plural)

8   Domestic, not foreign. (adjective; can also be a noun) The .... Office looks after domestic policy.

9   Money given to those in need of government help, e.g. unemployment .... (noun; can also be a verb)

10   A law passed by Parliament. (noun; can also be a verb)

12   A draft (working version, for discussion) of no. 10. (noun; can also be a verb)

13   Violent disturbance by people protesting about something. (noun; can also be a verb)

6 Report-writing

Your boss / colleague / overseas team member was unable to attend your last meeting. Write a short report on how successful the meeting was and what was decided. Alternatively, you may prefer to write a report on the meeting on page 24 of the Student's Book.

7 Second conditionals

Complete the sentences. Be as inventive as you wish!

1 If job-sharing was introduced into my company, ...

2 Money wouldn't be so important if ....

3 I would work much better if ....

4 Life would be much simpler if ....

5 If I hadn't joined this company, ...

6 I would have started to study English earlier if ....

7 When I was younger, if I had known what I know now I ....

8 I would have had more opportunities if ....

8 Reducing unemployment

The following measures to reduce unemployment are described on page 24 of the Student's Book:

A job-sharing   **B** compulsory sabbaticals   **C** four-day week

Now look at this list of points in support of the three measures. Decide which point could be used to support each measure.

1 Easy to implement in the civil service, schools, and factories. ....

2 Would enable people to travel / renovate their houses / dedicate more time to themselves and their families. ....

3 Would help people to get out of usual routine and regain enthusiasm. They would return to work refreshed and with new ideas. ....

4 If one employee changed jobs, then the other would be available to teach the new employee. ....

5 Less need to miss work for doctor's visits, etc. ....

6 More free time to dedicate to family / house / car maintenance. ....

7 More opportunities for voluntary service. ....

8 Reduction in exhaust emissions from commuter cars. ....

9 Would resolve problem of replacing people when they're ill. ....

10 Suitable for almost any kind of job. ....

11 Long weekends and shorter holidays. ....

12 The leisure industry would benefit from having potentially quite rich people with a lot of free time on their hands. ....

13 Two heads are better than one – new ideas for doing the job better might come up. Responsibilities would be shared. ....

14 Younger people would have a greater chance to succeed. ....

3 ORGANIZATION

1 Organizational culture

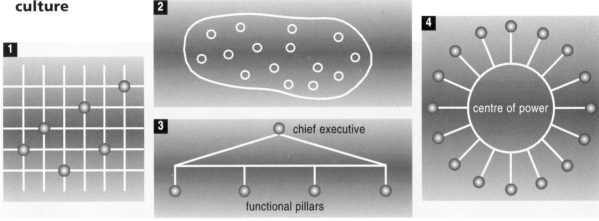

1 Insert the words in the box into the text below. Which organizational model above does the text refer to?

band	dovetailed	format	markets	standpoint
benefit	firms	generated	overriding	welfare

The 'people / person' culture exists for the people in it, where a group has decided that it is in their own ....[1] interests to ....[2] together, and to produce an organization for their ....[3]. It may be found in certain research groups; a university department; music, rock, and jazz groups; family ....[4]; and companies started by groups of friends, where the first coming together is ....[5] by the people involved rather than the matter in hand. There is little formal organization or structure, total flexibility, total interest in the work, total interest in the mutual ....[6] and benefits of all those concerned.

Such organizations will exist in this ....[7], or from this ....[8], for a short period only. In the interests of permanence and continuity, and prosperity and success, the initial coming together of people must be ....[9] with attention to task, ...[10], invention, and sales.

2 Now write a short paragraph describing one of the other two models presented above, and what you think the advantages and disadvantages of such a structure are.

2 How well do you know your company?

First answer the questions, then use your answers as the basis for writing a short description of your company and its activities.

1 How long ago was it founded? By whom?

....

2 Are any of the founding members still working?

....

3 How many people are employed by the company?

....

4 How many branches are there?

....

5 Do you have any offices abroad?

....

6 What has the profit curve looked like in the last five years?

....

7 Which are your best selling products / services?

....

8 Have these products / services always been the best selling ones?

....

9 What is this year's expected revenue? How does that compare with last year?

....

10 What are the short-, mid-, and long-term plans for the company?

....

3 Useful phrases: general

1 Match a word from **1–5** with another from **a–e** to make a new word or phrase. Then do the same with **6–10** and **f–j**.

1	retail	a	objective
2	strategic	b	manager
3	corporate	c	sharing
4	middle	d	strategy
5	information	e	trade
6	work	f	date
7	net	g	force
8	turn	h	working
9	back	i	house
10	ware	j	over

2 Now match the phrasal and prepositional verbs (**1–5**) with their meanings (**a–f**). Then do the same with **6–10** and **f–j**.

1	branch out	a	deviate from main subject
2	drift off	b	be accountable to a superior
3	report to	c	be in essence
4	boil down to	d	be occupied with
5	deal with	e	expand business into new areas
6	look out	f	take care of
7	look after	g	be careful
8	look up to	h	admire
9	look into	i	anticipate with pleasure
10	look forward to	j	investigate

4 Do you have executive potential?

1 One of your staff comes to you with some small idea for increasing efficiency. You had already thought of the idea and are preparing to put it into effect.

  a Tell them* that you have already thought of the idea, but do appreciate the suggestion.

  b Say nothing about your prior conception, but simply praise them for their co-operation.

  c Neither **a** nor **b**.

2 Your department has a series of important tasks to perform involving complicated procedures. You feel your experience means you are the best person to carry them out.

  a Take the time to attend to every detail personally.

  b Plan to delegate where possible to subordinates.

  c Neither **a** nor **b**.

3 You are trying to get a stubborn associate to proceed with your idea or suggestion.

  a If possible, try to present the idea in such a way that they feel it emerges, at least partly, from their brain.

  b Make certain that you get full credit for the idea.

  c Neither **a** nor **b**.

4 You know that one of your prospective customers collects butterflies.

  a Before a business meeting, you produce a butterfly specimen and say, 'By the way, I've heard that you're an expert on butterflies. My youngster caught this one, and I've saved it to ask you what kind it is.'

  b You don't do anything as showing undue interest might be considered presumptuous.

  c Neither **a** nor **b**.

* It is becoming increasingly common, especially in spoken English, to substitute *them* for the repetitive *him / her*.

5 *job* vs *work*

Put the verbs in brackets into the correct tense (past simple, present perfect simple, present perfect continuous). Change the word order where necessary. Underline *job* or *work* as appropriate.

1 Since you arrived at *job / work* this morning (you make) .... one mistake after another – what's got in to you?

2 (She finally reach) .... a decision. She's going to take that new *job / work* – isn't that good news?

3 (You do) .... anything interesting last weekend? (I just do) .... a few *jobs / works* around the house.

4 What (you do) .... all morning? It's already 11.30 and (you not do) .... any *job / work* yet.

5 (I do) .... my homework. (I already finish) .... six exercises, only one more to go, but it's hard *job / work*.

6 Pronunciation

(1) Write these words in the correct row according to their pronunciation.

core	pair	sir
fare	play	square
her	pour	they
law	raw	they're

/ɜː/
were ....

/ɔː/
wore ....

/eə/
where ....

/eɪ/
weigh ....

2 Write *S* or *Z* next to the following words depending on how the *s* is pronounced.
e.g. plays *Z* house *S*

1 absolute ....   8 busy ....   15 praise ....

2 advertise ....   9 earnings ....   16 purpose ....

3 analyse ....   10 enclose ....   17 release ....

4 answer ....   11 lease ....   18 reserve ....

5 appraise ....   12 means ....   19 resource ....

6 bonus ....   13 opposite ....   20 towards ....

7 browse ....   14 pleasant ....

---

7 Education word search

In the word search are 23 subjects studied at college and university. You only need to work in three directions: left to right, diagonally top left to bottom right, and top to bottom. Can you find them all?

A	R	C	H	I	T	E	C	T	U	R	E	D
E	G	S	B	I	O	L	O	G	Y	M	C	R
G	N	R	O	U	S	M	E	D	I	A	O	A
E	X	G	I	C	S	T	X	A	R	T	M	M
O	P	E	I	C	I	I	O	X	X	H	P	A
G	C	O	X	N	U	O	N	R	X	S	U	X
R	L	L	L	P	E	L	L	E	Y	X	T	E
A	A	O	M	I	H	E	T	O	S	X	I	C
P	S	G	X	U	T	Y	R	U	G	S	N	O
H	S	Y	X	X	S	I	S	I	R	Y	G	L
Y	I	X	M	E	D	I	C	I	N	E	L	O
E	C	O	N	O	M	I	C	S	C	G	A	G
X	S	L	A	N	G	U	A	G	E	S	W	Y

Of the subjects you found in the word search, which do you find:
- most interesting?
- most boring?
- most useful for the 21st century?
- least useful?

4 NUMBERS

1 The story of numbers

Look at the pictures of the ancient writing systems. Match the captions below with the pictures.

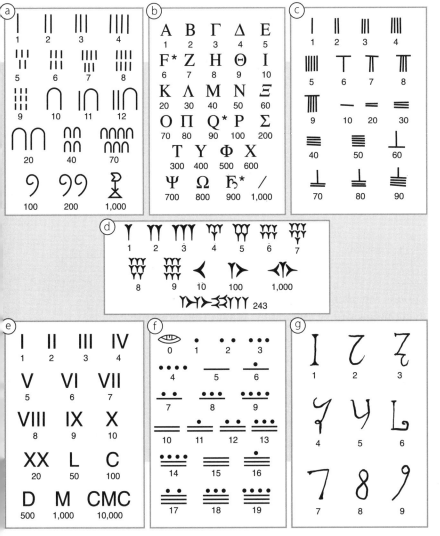

1 Babylonian cuneiform writing: a big advance on the sticks and stones used by primitive man.

2 Ancient Egyptian hieroglyphic system: a purely additive system.

3 Ancient Greek: numbers consisted of letters of the alphabet plus three symbols indicated by asterisks here.

4 Ancient Chinese place system: a number symbol took on different values according to the place it occupied in the written number.

5 Tenth century Arabic numerals: system originated in India, adopted by Arabs and then spread to Europe. By the fifteenth century, numbers had their current form.

6 Maya 20-base system: this enabled Mayans to create the most accurate calendars in pre-Hispanic America. Unlike most other civilizations they had a zero, represented by a kind of shell.

7 Roman letter system: if a number was smaller than the number that followed it, it was subtracted from the second number; if it was as large or larger than the following number, the second number was added to the first.

2 Prepositions

Insert prepositions into the spaces where necessary.

1 There has been a rise .... 10%.

2 There has been a 10% .... rise .... sales.

3 The top income tax bracket has been raised .... 66% .... 84%.

4 There has been a steady fall .... the birth rate of some European countries.

5 Six thousand .... dollars was spent on training in the first month.

6 At the turn of the century the figure stood .... 4.2, the same .... now.

7 One .... two (1:2) people in this company cannot speak English.

8 The proportion of attendees who can't speak English is one .... five (1:5).

---

3 _one_ vs _a / an_   Underline one or both of the words.

1   If you make _a / one_ mistake, a dialogue window appears on your screen.

2   _A / One_ possible way to do this is to set out some strategic objectives.

3   We only did _an / one_ experiment before the apparatus exploded.

4   Can you give me _a / one_ breakdown of costs please?

5   There are at least _a / one_ hundred manual operators in our workforce.

6   I thought there were two hundred not _a / one_ hundred.

7   _A / One_ man called for you this morning, but he didn't leave his name.

8   We can decide from _a / one_ week to the next.

9   _A / One_ quarter of those interviewed said they did it _a time / one time / once_ a week.

10   I'll have _a / one_ beer please.

---

4 Countable or uncountable?   Some uncountable nouns can also be countable, but their meaning changes. Which of the following nouns can be countable? What do they mean?

baggage	furniture	interest	money
coffee	hair	jeans	paper
energy	hardware	knowledge	scissors
expertise	help	machinery	traffic
evidence	homework	mathematics	work

---

5 Singular or plural?   Underline the correct form.

1   Juventus _is / are_ one of the richest football clubs in Europe.

2   Real Madrid _is / are_ playing Juventus tomorrow night.

3   If there _is / are_ more than one possible answer, then choose the most appropriate.

4   Up to 40% of funds _is / are_ deposited in banks.

5   Three hundred _doesn't / don't_ sound too high.

6   Two thirds of those interviewed _say / says_ that they don't agree.

7   The maximum allowance _is / are_ twenty-four kilos.

8   Twenty-four kilos _is / are_ quite heavy.

9   A set of golf clubs _cost / costs_ $2,500.

10   A couple of hours _is / are_ not long to wait.

6 Articles

Insert *a / an*, *the*, or nothing into the spaces below.

..........¹ Pentium chip had ....² 'bug'. Intel had known about it for some time but had treated it as ....³ technical problem. They had taken ....⁴ engineering perspective rather than ....⁵ customer-public relations one, despite ....⁶ fact that they had gone ....⁷ long way in ....⁸ previous years towards recreating themselves as ....⁹ marketing company.

..........¹⁰ computer chip is not very interesting in itself, but ....¹¹ 'power at ....¹² heart of ....¹³ your business', certainly is, and their slogan 'Intel inside' was ....¹⁴ clever statement of this. Intel decided that as ....¹⁵ bug was such ....¹⁶ small fault and statistically almost negligible, they did not have to worry about it, and therefore neither would their customers. Wrong! When ....¹⁷ problem came to ....¹⁸ light, Intel issued ....¹⁹ statement that ....²⁰ basic spreadsheet users would hit ....²¹ error once every 27,000 years. This was absolutely accurate but did little to allay customer disquiet.

..........²² Intel competitors were not slow to point out that ....²³ risk would be greatly increased for ....²⁴ financial analyst who uses ....²⁵ spreadsheets most of ....²⁶ day, and this is precisely ....²⁷ person who cannot afford to make ....²⁸ error. Also, ...²⁹ normal users do not use ....³⁰ random floating point values that Intel used to illustrate ....³¹ problem of error. They use ....³² other calculations that would increase ....³³ chance of ....³⁴ mistake. Intel had analysed ....³⁵ statistics, but did nothing to calm ....³⁶ fears of ....³⁷ customers, who were uninterested in ....³⁸ statistical analyses or ....³⁹ theoretical chances of error.

Their perception was that of ....⁴⁰ car owner who finds that there is ....⁴¹ design fault in ....⁴² engine that means there is ....⁴³ risk of ....⁴⁴ crash – ....⁴⁵ totally unacceptable situation. ....⁴⁶ survey in ....⁴⁷ USA at ....⁴⁸ time quoted ....⁴⁹ average consumer comment: 'I am not sure what ....⁵⁰ Pentium is, but I know something is wrong with it.' Bad news for Intel, who to their public relations credit, but accounting debit, set about recalling and replacing all faulty chips.

7 Money word search

Make sure you know the meanings of the words in the box and then find them in the word search. You can work in any direction.

~~beg~~	fare	money	savings
bill	fine	price	tax
cash	fund	pay	tip
coin	income	rate	token
cost	inflation	revenue	wage
exchange	interest	salary	

Y	I	N	T	E	R	E	S	T	E
E	C	N	Z	X	C	S	I	X	M
N	O	Z	F	I	A	P	C	A	O
O	I	U	R	L	S	H	R	T	C
M	N	P	A	L	A	E	P	A	N
D	F	R	L	N	V	T	S	A	I
F	Y	I	G	E	I	H	I	C	Y
A	B	E	N	Z	N	E	K	O	T
R	Z	U	Z	E	G	E	B	S	N
E	E	G	A	W	S	R	A	T	E

8 Word stress

All the words below have two syllables. Which pattern do they follow? Write *1* if they have the stress on the first syllable (e.g. **thir**ty = *1*), or *2* on the second syllable (e.g. thir**teen** = *2*).

1 assets ....
2 budget ....
3 business ....
4 colleague ....
5 command ....
6 complex ....
7 concept ....
8 consist ....
9 contents ....
10 control ....

11 correct ....
12 credit ....
13 current ....
14 defect ....
15 event ....
16 factor ....
17 foreign ....
18 forecast ....
19 income ....
20 logo ....

21 outlet ....
22 per cent ....
23 product ....
24 profit ....
25 response ....
26 restrict ....
27 result ....
28 return ....
29 survey ....
30 towards ....

9 Pronunciation

Do the vowels in the pairs of words have the same pronunciation? Put a tick (✓) beside those which do.

1   measure / decimal ....

2   meter / metric ....

3   minus / size ....

4   nought / thousand ....

5   number / numerical ....

6   plus / hundred ....

7   quarter / square ....

8   third / first ....

9   weight / height ....

10   zero / pair ....

10 Number games

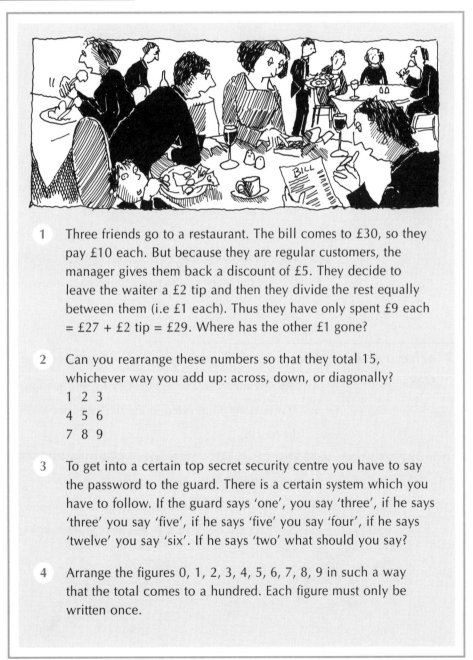

1   Three friends go to a restaurant. The bill comes to £30, so they pay £10 each. But because they are regular customers, the manager gives them back a discount of £5. They decide to leave the waiter a £2 tip and then they divide the rest equally between them (i.e £1 each). Thus they have only spent £9 each = £27 + £2 tip = £29. Where has the other £1 gone?

2   Can you rearrange these numbers so that they total 15, whichever way you add up: across, down, or diagonally?
1 2 3
4 5 6
7 8 9

3   To get into a certain top secret security centre you have to say the password to the guard. There is a certain system which you have to follow. If the guard says 'one', you say 'three', if he says 'three' you say 'five', if he says 'five' you say 'four', if he says 'twelve' you say 'six'. If he says 'two' what should you say?

4   Arrange the figures 0, 1, 2, 3, 4, 5, 6, 7, 8, 9 in such a way that the total comes to a hundred. Each figure must only be written once.

11 Comparisons

Write out the numbers / measurements in **bold** in full. Fill in the gaps with the superlative of the following adjectives, and use each adjective only once (though *highest* may appear to belong to more than one sentence).

early	fast	heavy	high	small

1   The .... known official honour is the 'Gold of Honour' awarded during the 18th dynasty in Egypt (**c. 1440–1400** BC) for extraordinary valour.

....

2   The tip of the .... thermometer (for measuring the temperature of single living cells) is one micron in diameter, about **$1/50$** the diameter of a human hair.

....

3   The .... baby on record is a boy of **10.2 kg (22 lb 8 oz)** born in **1955**.

....

4   The .... speed at which human beings have travelled is **39,897 km/h** aboard the Apollo 10.

....

5   The country with the .... divorce rate is America where it is about **1:2** (i.e. for every two marriages one ends in divorce).

....

12 *arise, raise, rise*

Insert *arise, raise,* or *rise* into the blank spaces and in an appropriate active tense.

1   Net revenue .... steadily for the last four years.

2   Transactions plummeted in the third quarter and then .... steeply in the fourth.

3   This .... an interesting question – what are the main threats to us doing business in overseas markets?

4   A wide array of issues .... at the meeting last week.

5   (You) .... your prices next year? Yes, but only marginally, not substantially.

5 COMMUNICATION

1 Telephone dialogue

Complete the dialogue with statements or questions.

RECEPTIONIST (*name of your company*) Good morning.

CALLER This is Penny O'Reilly speaking. Could I speak to Mr Smith please?

RECEPTIONIST ....¹?

CALLER O'Reilly. From Hardwick Software.

RECEPTIONIST ....²?

CALLER No, it's OK. I can wait a couple of minutes.

RECEPTIONIST ....³?

CALLER I said I could wait a couple of minutes.

RECEPTIONIST ....⁴.

CALLER OK. Could you ask him to call me back?

RECEPTIONIST ....⁵.

CALLER Yes he has, but I'll give you it anyway. It's 0171–980–4167.

RECEPTIONIST ....⁶?

CALLER Yes, of course.

RECEPTIONIST ....⁷.

CALLER No, its 4167, not 76.

RECEPTIONIST ....⁸?

CALLER Any time before 5.00 our time.

RECEPTIONIST ....⁹.

CALLER Thank you very much. Goodbye.

2 Useful phrases: letter writing

Number the phrases according to these headings:

A The beginning
B Explaining the purpose
C Requesting information
D Giving information or replying to a request for information
E Apologizing
F The closing

1 Further to … ....

2 We have received your letter of (*date*) in which you asked … ....

3 Could you please …? ....

4 Please do not hesitate to contact us should you need any further information. ....

5 We are extremely sorry to hear about the problem. ....

6 Thank you for your letter of (*date*). ....

7 Please find enclosed … ……….

8 We would like to enquire about / whether … ……….

9 We look forward to meeting / hearing from you in the near future. ……….

10 We very much regret that this problem has happened. ……….

---

3 Indirect speech Put the following sentences into indirect speech, using a suitable verb.

1 Could I speak to Mr Jones please?

....

2 Sorry, I didn't quite catch that.

....

3 I think you must have dialled the wrong number.

....

4 I'm afraid she no longer works here.

....

5 Sorry, where are you calling from?

....

6 Would you like to hold the line or shall I get Ms Smith to ring you back?

....

7 I'm afraid Ms Green has just left the office. She should be back in half an hour.

....

8 I'll just check that for you.

....

9 Shall I spell that for you?

....

10 Sorry to keep you. Hope you haven't been waiting long.

....

4 Linking words

1 One of the four words in each group has no connection with the others. Which one?

a	as regards	in relation to	in connection with	in addition to
b	for example	e.g.	in fact	such as
c	in addition	moreover	furthermore	despite
d	whereas	thus	therefore	consequently
e	since	although	as	seeing as
f	yet	but	however	likewise
g	also	as well	conversely	too
h	owing to	as a result of	apart from	due to
i	in summary	specifically	in brief	to sum up
j	alternatively	finally	lastly	in conclusion

2 Now complete the letter underlining the correct word / phrase in the boxes.

Dear Mr Kronos

We thank you for your letter of 8 March 2090 *in connection with / in addition to* [1] our order for ten time machines.

Due to / Apart from [2] unforeseen circumstances, we will be obliged to reduce our order from ten to five machines. We would *also / as well* [3] ask you to extend our credit for an extra 90 days. *Alternatively / Finally* [4], we could wait three months and then re-order.

We are extremely sorry for any inconvenience this will cause you. *But / However* [5], we feel that *as / although* [6] we have been customers of yours for nearly 30 years, you are sure to understand our situation given the current galactic climate.

Whereas / Therefore [7] we would ask you kindly to cancel our original order and inform your bank to credit our account.

Finally / In summary [8], we would like to say once again how impressed we are with your new line of machines and with your discovery of parallel time zones.

We look forward to hearing from you in the near future.

Yours sincerely

USE A PARALLEL TIME ZONE AND DELIVER THIS LETTER YESTERDAY.

5 **Keyboard**   Can you match the keys with their names?

1	ampersand	12	apostrophe
2	asterisk	13	colon
3	at	14	comma
4	dash	15	curly brackets / parentheses
5	exclamation mark	16	full stop / period / point / dot
6	hyphen	17	semicolon
7	number	18	single / double quotation marks / inverted commas
8	per cent	19	square brackets / parentheses
9	round brackets / parentheses	20	back slash
10	tilde	21	forward slash
11	angled brackets / parentheses		

6 How well are you communicating?

Check out what kind of relationship you have with your partner by choosing one answer for each of the questions below. Then look at your score.

1 Your partner asks your opinion of a meal he / she has prepared for you. What do you say?
   a Say it is delicious and praise his / her efforts.
   b Tell the truth at all costs.
   c Say it would probably have been cheaper to eat out.

2 If you have been watching a TV play or documentary together, what happens afterwards?
   a You both voice your opinions even if you don't agree.
   b You try to avoid a discussion since you already know his / her viewpoint.
   c You seldom enjoy watching the same type of programme.

3 Your partner has a habit, such as smoking, which you hate.
   a Tell him / her how happy it would make you if he / she could give it up.
   b Threaten him / her with dire consequences if he / she continues.
   c Flush his / her cigarettes down the toilet.

WELL THERE'S NO RIVER MARKED ON THE MAP.

4 What are most of your disagreements about?
   a Small matters easily resolved.   c Basic misunderstandings.
   b Money.

5 Navigating new territory, your partner, who is driving, takes a wrong turn. What do you do?
   a Get out the map and trace a new route.
   b Pretend not to notice you are going the wrong way.
   c Sit back smugly, and tell him / her what a fool he / she is.

6 On your birthday, your lover buys you something you don't like. What do you say?
   a Thank him / her for the gift and comment on his / her general kindness.
   b Tell him / her honestly the damaging truth.
   c Say it's about time he / she knew what you wanted.

Time to take action!

0–3:   Disastrous. Oh dear! It appears that your ability to communicate is not all it might be.

4–6:   Less than satisfactory. You are not giving as much time to communicating effectively as these lead to slight misunderstandings.

7–9:   Reasonable. Yours is a fairly typical relationship; for the most part you understand and empathize with each other, but there are occasional lapses (probably on both sides) and you should consider ways of improving it!

10–12: Excellent. You appear to have a very warm and effective level of communication with your partner and the betting is that your relationship is a very happy and comfortable one.

Score: 2 points for every (a), one point for (b), and no points for (c).

6 TRAVEL

1 Ten travel tips Read the tips for Americans preparing a business trip abroad. Mark * those tips that you already follow, and + those that you think would be a good idea to follow. Finally, thinking back to your last business trip, write one of the two letters outlined in point 10.

▶ **1** Order an extra supply of business cards.

▶ **2** Set up your appointments weeks and months in advance and have them confirmed in writing. Unlike Americans, business people overseas do not check into a hotel and start making telephone calls for appointments.

▶ **3** Get a list of national and religious holidays around the world. You won't be able to conduct business on a day, or during a period, when a country is celebrating a holiday.

▶ **4** Arm yourself with the U.S. State Department's Background Notes for each country you plan to visit. These are chock full of information on the history, form of government, economics, demographics, and other helpful information.

▶ **5** If at all possible, fly business class to any destination that requires more than four hours' flying time. The need to arrive as fresh and rested as possible is especially important in business.

▶ **6** Investigate the ATA Carnet system if you are planning to carry along commercial samples, advertising material, audiovisual material, medical or scientific equipment, or other tools of your trade. The United States is a member of this system, which permits business travelers to carry these materials into a country for temporary periods without paying duties, taxes, or posting a bond.

▶ **7** Dress conservatively.

▶ **8** Consider stowing away a few general purpose gifts.

▶ **9** Have any sales literature and price lists you plan to carry and distribute translated into the local language before you leave home.

▶ **10** Write two types of letters upon your return home to contacts you have made overseas.

   a Thank-you notes for people who assisted or hosted you.
   b Letters of confirmation to cover any agreements or general understandings you made.

---

2 Future trips

Circle the correct future form, and underline *journey*, *travel*, or *trip*.

1 Will you *see / be seeing* Patricia tomorrow? If you are, will you *ask / be asking* her what the *travel / trip* arrangements are?

2 OK. I'll *see / be seeing* Mr Erman and tell him what we've decided about the *travel / trip*.

3 It's really no problem. I'll *go / be going* past the station myself anyway so it won't *make / be making* my *journey / travel* any longer.

4 If you can't find anyone else for this business *journey / travel / trip* then I'll *have / be having* to ask you I'm afraid.

5 I don't think I'll *arrive / be arriving* until after midnight – the train connections are really bad, so the *journey / trip / travel* will *take / be taking* about six hours.

---

3 Giving directions

Reply to this fax.

> Dear (your name)
> I forgot to ask you how to get to your office from the nearest airport. I'll be renting a car at the airport, so perhaps you could fax me a map with a few written instructions on how to reach you. It'll certainly feel strange driving on the other (the wrong!) side of the road! Looking forward to seeing you, and let's hope we can wind things up this time.
> Best wishes
> Jo

---

4 Buying a rail ticket

You are making enquiries about a return trip to London from another station in England. The cost of train tickets in the UK varies depending on the time of day you're travelling – *peak* (i.e. rush hour when most people are going to work) or *off-peak*. It also depends on when you buy your ticket. Read the complete dialogue before filling in the spaces.

YOU ....[1]?

CLERK It depends what time you are travelling.

YOU ....[2].

CLERK Well, in that case, because you'll be leaving after 11.00 you can get the reduced fare, which is £55, provided that you book twenty-four hours in advance.

YOU ....[3]?

CLERK You can come back on any off-peak train within the next month.

YOU   ....⁴?

CLERK   Yes, of course, we accept all major credit cards.

YOU   ....⁵?

CLERK   No, it's a direct train straight through to
        London Euston.

YOU   ....⁶?

CLERK   Normally from platform three.

---

5 What do you say when ...?

Write what you would say to the relevant person in the following airport situations.

e.g. The ground hostess tells you that your suitcases are 20 kilos over the limit.

   Will I have to pay excess baggage?

1   You want a seat in non-smoking.

   ....

2   You hear an announcement. You're not sure if it was for your flight.

   ....

3   You lose your boarding card some time between passport control and going to your gate.

   ....

4   The person sitting next to you on the plane is reading an interesting article that you would very much like to read too.

   ....

5   You don't understand how to operate the public telephones.

   ....

6   You don't know where the car rental agencies are.

   ....

7   You want to ask a taxi driver the cost to get to the Hilton Hotel.

   ....

8   You want to give the taxi driver a tip.

   ....

6 Car parts

There are about sixty differences between British and American English with regard to parts of the car. Look at the picture below; the parts of the car are identified with their British names.

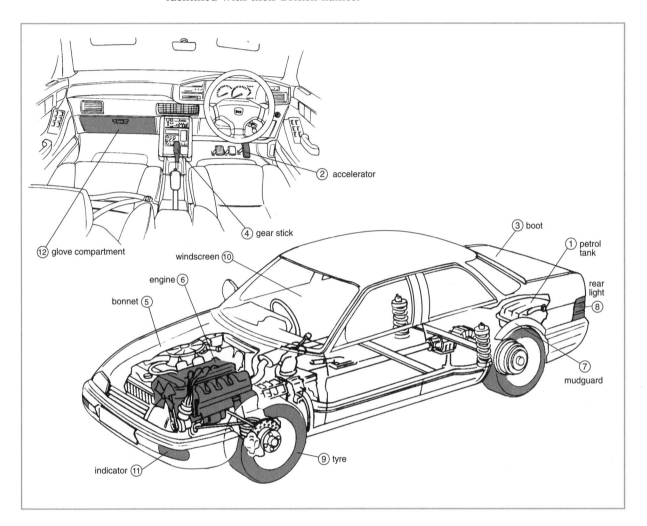

Now match these American part names with their English equivalents numbered in the diagram.

a   fender (enclosure over the wheels)
b   gas tank (where you put the fuel)
c   gear shift (for changing gears)
d   hood (the engine is underneath this)
e   motor (the main machine in a car)
f   tail lights (the ones at the back of the car)
g   tire (pronounced the same as in British English, but spelt differently)
h   trunk (where you put your luggage, shopping etc.)
i   turn signals (these indicate if you're turning left or right)
j   windshield (the glass in front of you)
k   gas pedal (this increases speed)
l   glove box (where you can keep small items)

7 Travel vocabulary: USA vs UK

Do you know the American equivalents of these British words connected with travel? Complete the puzzle to find them. A key word (number 10) will be revealed when you have completed the puzzle. What is its equivalent in British English?

lorry	crossroads	motorway
flyover	pavement	petrol
tube / underground	car	road surface

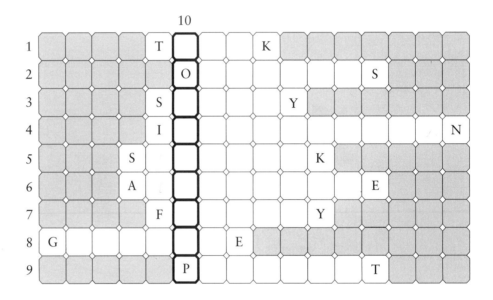

8 Opposites

What are the opposites to these words (in relation to travel and directions)?

e.g. leave *arrive*

1 arrival ....

2 on time ....

3 nearest ....

4 single / one way (tickets) ....

5 to take off ....

6 to get on (public transport) ....

7 to get in (cars) ....

8 behind ....

9 automatic (cars) ....

10 (Is this seat) free? ....

7 PLANNING

1 Rules of economics?

Below are ten principles of economics. Insert the words and phrases in the box into the correct spaces. Do you agree with any or all of the principles?

economic	margin	rise	trade	inflation
give up	incentives	outcomes	standard	tradeoffs

1 People face ....

2 The cost of something is what you .... to get it.

3 Rational people think at the ....

4 People respond to ....

5 .... can make everyone better off.

6 Markets are usually a good way to organize .... activity.

7 Governments can sometimes improve market ....

8 A country's .... of living depends on its ability to produce goods and services.

9 Prices .... when the government prints too much money.

10 Society faces a short-run tradeoff between .... and unemployment.

2 Silent letters

In each of the words one of the letters is 'silent'. Which one? How is each word pronounced?

e.g. knee __k__ /niː/

1 resign ....

2 business ....

3 aisle ....

4 suit ....

5 knob ....

6 knowledge ....

7 calm ....

8 science ....

9 guarantee ....

10 debt ....

3 Stress

Underline the stressed syllables, and mark the pairs of words according to whether they have the stress on the same syllable (write *S*) or a different syllable (*D*).

e.g. corres<u>pond</u>, corres<u>pon</u>dence   *S* ....

comm<u>u</u>nicate, communi<u>ca</u>tion   *D* ....

1   applicant / application ....

2   attend / attendee ....

3   available / availability ....

4   compete / competitive ....

5   economic / economical ....

6   efficient / efficiency ....

7   engine / engineer ....

8   feasible / feasibility ....

9   hypothesis / hypothetical ....

10   liable / liability ....

11   machine / machinery ....

12   method / methodology ....

13   production / productivity ....

14   profit / profitable ....

15   reliable / reliability ....

16   sequence / sequential ....

17   standard / standardize ....

18   strategy / strategic ....

19   technique / technical ....

20   theory / theoretical ....

4 Future simple and future perfect

Choose a year / week / month, underline the correct form of the verb in *italics*, and complete the sentences or circle a suitable word or phrase.

e.g. Next (week) / month / year I will *finish* / <u>*have finished*</u> my report / my current project / (this exercise).

1   In 2010 / 2015 / 2020 / 2030 I will *be* / *have been* .... years of age.

2   In 2010 / 2015 / 2020 / 2030 I will *work* / *have worked* for a total of .... years.

3   By 2010 / 2015 / 2020 / 2030 I will *reach* / *have reached* the position of ....

4   By 2010 / 2015 / 2020 / 2030 I will *achieve* / *have achieved* some / nearly all / all of my ambitions.

5   Next week / month / year I will probably *get* / *have got* promoted / the sack / married.

6   Next week / month / year I will *stop* / *have stopped* doing .... and *start* / *have started* doing ....

7   By next week / month / year my level of English will *be* / *have been* ....

5 Environment word search

One of the biggest problems humanity faces in the 21st century is planning how to save the environment and animals from extinction. Check you know the meanings of the following words and then find them in the word search. You can work in three directions only: left to right, top left to bottom right diagonally, and top to bottom.

B	J	I	S	F	U	R	F	W	A	S	T	E
A	I	S	N	K	X	V	O	O	I	L	P	G
A	I	O	C	S	I	S	R	O	C	T	D	R
O	T	R	D	G	E	N	E	D	O	Z	E	E
W	Z	M	P	E	L	C	S	A	A	G	S	E
H	I	O	O	O	G	E	T	P	L	B	T	N
A	U	L	N	S	L	R	X	I	R	R	R	H
L	M	N	D	E	P	L	A	T	C	A	O	O
E	E	I	T	L	L	H	U	D	I	I	Y	U
P	L	A	N	T	I	A	E	T	A	N	D	S
A	C	I	D	K	X	F	Y	R	I	B	C	E
X	R	E	C	Y	C	L	E	E	E	O	L	T
R	E	S	O	U	R	C	E	S	R	W	N	E

acid	oil
air	~~ozone~~
atmosphere	plant
biodegradeable	pond
coal	pollution
destroy	rainbow
extinct	recycle
forest	resources
fur	seal
greenhouse	skin
hunt	spray
insecticide	waste
layer	whale
lead	wildlife
mink	wood

6 Writing

Using this information, reply to this e-mail summarizing your plans for a future visit.

To	From
Judy Clarke	Henri Fourde
j.clarke@meta4.co.uk	h.fourde@modelt.fr

Subject

Visit

Hi Judy
Just a quick note to confirm that the offer's still open for you to come and see our new production line in action. It should be operative from the beginning of next month, so any time after then would be fine. If you fancy bringing your husband along too and making a weekend of it then that would be great.
Hope to hear from you soon.
Henri

BRITISH AIRWAYS

Boarding Pass
Carte d'accès à bord
Einsteigekarte
Tarjeta de embarque

BOARDING PASS

J. Clarke
London to Paris

Passenger Ticket and Baggage Check

IATA

:3426:737:439

Subject to conditions of contract in this ticket

The ticket is not valid and will not be accepted for carriage unless purchased from the issuing carrier or its authorized travel agent

7 Business plans

Complete the crossword, and decide which of the factors affects (most and least) your company's plans for the future.

1   Tendencies to develop in a particular direction.
2   How a company (or other entity) is organized.
3   Rivalry in business for customers or markets.
4   Positive possible courses of actions.
5   The opposite of strengths.
6   A way of living of people / society.
7   The opposite of weaknesses.
8   Imminent dangers which might jeopardize business.
9   What a company offers its clients in terms of maintenance, requirements, support etc.
10   The area of knowledge that applies science to commerce and industry.

8 PRODUCTS

1 Reading

Ever thought that machines had a mind of their own? Read on!

Warning!

This machine is prone to breaking down during periods of heavy use.

The machine has a circuit which detects the state of mind of the person attempting to use it, and reacts in proportion to the urgency of the situation. The more desperate the operator becomes, the more likely the machine is to malfunction. Violence on the part of the operator may cause it to break down altogether. Attempting to use a different machine will only cause the malfunction to spread; they belong to the same union.

The only solution is to stay calm, say something soothing, and refrain from hitting it. Never let a machine know you are in a hurry.

IT KNOWS YOU DON'T LIKE IT. IT WON'T WORK IF IT'S FRIGHTENED.

2 Word stress

In which cases is the stress <u>not</u> the same on all three words? The first word in each group is a verb.

1	consume	consumer	consumption
2	customize	customer	custom
3	develop	developer	development
4	direct	director	direction
5	economize	economist	economy
6	employ	employee	employment
7	govern	governor	government
8	install	installer	installation
9	interpret	interpreter	interpretation
10	invest	investor	investment
11	manage	manager	management
12	negotiate	negotiator	negotiation
13	organize	organizer	organization
14	perform	performer	performance
15	project	projector	projection

3 Devices word search

Check you know the meanings of the following 20 words and then find them in the word search (you can work in any direction, up, down, diagonally, left to right, right to left).

B	A	T	T	E	R	Y	W	I	R	E
E	A	P	P	L	I	A	N	C	E	F
C	C	S	P	X	X	O	T	S	S	A
I	P	I	E	A	Z	H	S	N	O	C
R	L	X	V	Z	R	A	W	O	C	I
C	A	B	L	E	L	A	I	T	K	L
U	S	E	A	G	D	X	T	T	E	I
I	T	D	V	P	I	H	C	U	T	T
T	I	E	L	D	N	A	H	B	S	Y
X	C	O	N	V	E	Y	O	R	X	X

apparatus	facility
appliance	glass
base	handle
battery	nozzle
button	plastic
cable	socket
chip	switch
circuit	thread
conveyor	valve
device	wire

4 The passive

Convert the following sentences into the passive.

1 The company is making plans for the future.

....

2 We have already told you twice.

....

3 I'll finish it by the end of the day.

....

4 You must do this before 12.00.

....

5 They saw him leaving the building.

....

5 Useful phrases: general business

Match a word from the first column (1–5) with a word in the second (a–e) to create a new word / phrase. Then do the same with 6–10 and f–j. Now check with your dictionary before looking at the key.

1	smart	a	study	6	short	f	stone
2	public	b	sourcing	7	mile	g	coming
3	break	c	even	8	dead	h	over
4	feasibility	d	relations	9	turn	i	down
5	out	e	materials	10	break	j	line

6 Test your mechanical aptitude

Fill in the missing spaces with words from the box below, choose the correct forms of the words in *italics*, and then choose the correct answer from the three alternatives.

Question 1: arrow, as, as, cause, counterclockwise, diagram, drives, drives, to, turns

Question 2: because, clockwise, follows, or, since, since, so, spring, then, therefore

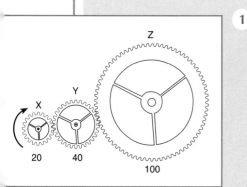

1   Assume that X, Y and Z in this ....[1] are gears. Gear X has 20 teeth, and ....[2] Gear Y. Gear Y has 40 teeth and ....[3] Gear Z. Gear Z has 100 teeth.

If X ....[4] in the direction shown by the ....[5], this will ....[6] Y to *move / move / moving*[7] in the:

a   same direction ....[8] the arrow.

b   opposite direction ....[9] the arrow.

c   partly in the same direction ....[10] the arrow, and partly ....[11].

2   Wheel A has 4 teeth and wheel B has 1 tooth. When not *be / being*[12] made *turn / to turn / turning*[13], B is snapped back to the original position by the pull of the steel ....[14] C.

..................[15]:

a   ....[16] A meshes with B, and ....[17] B cannot turn continuously ....[18] of the spring C, it ....[19] that A cannot turn continuously.

b   If wheel A turned ....[20] more than once, ...[21] either B would stretch the spring too far and ....[22] force the apparatus *stop / to stop / stopping*[23], ...[24] the spring would break under the tension.

c   A could keep turning, *cause / causing*[25] the tooth on B *move / to move / moving*[26] down and up 4 times to each revolution of A.

7 Writing

Write a description of one of the following processes:

- how to apply for residence (or divorce) in your country
- how the postal system works in all its facets
- how to become a top manager (or a billionaire).

8 *Chindogu*

1 Below is a Japanese *Chindogu*. Write down what you think it is and how it is used.

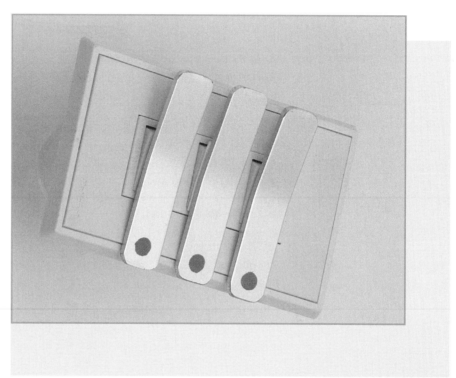

2 Now design your own *Chindogu*. Decide what its function is and how it works and write a short description.

9 VISITING

1 Pronunciation   List these words according to the pronunciation of *th*.

thank	algorithm	cloth
that	authority	length
theory	breathe	path
thesis	clothing	strength
thing	mathematics	twelfth
threshold	method	health
thus	without	with

/ð/ ....

....

/θ/ ....

....

2 Asking about a flight   A colleague has just arrived from England. These are his / her answers to some questions. What were the questions?

1 ....?

No, there was some turbulence, so it was rather bumpy.

2 ....?

No, there was a two-hour delay.

3 ....?

Just over four hours.

4 ....?

Well, no, not really, but the wine was OK.

5 ....?

At the Hilton.

6 ....?

Cloudy and wet, as usual.

3 Countries

Insert letters into the spaces to reveal the names of countries. Then write the nationality in the second column, and the name of the principal / official language spoken in each country in the third column.

	Country	Nationality	Language
1	......wede......		
2	......itzerlan......		
3	......urke......		
4	......enmar......		
5	......ustri......		
6	......exic......		
7	......gyp......		
8	......olan......		
9	......hailan......		
10	......ale......		

4 What do you say when ...?

Write down the words you would use in the following situations.

1   You arrive at your client's house. They immediately present you with a gift. You have nothing to give them in return.

....

2   Your host begins criticizing the politics of your country.

....

3   Your host asks you how much your house is worth.

....

4   Your host asks you how much money you earn.

....

5   You want to smoke.

....

6   You break an object in your host's house.

....

7   You've unwittingly said something to offend your guest.

....

8   Your guest is having trouble eating a complicated dish.

....

5 The 'American Way'

Insert the words and phrases in the box into the spaces.

> **1–7**: 'let's get down to business', fiscal quarter, frameworks, geared, getting the job done, goal structuring, short term
>
> **8–15**: deadlines, hierarchy, information exchange, measure, personal connections, schedules, seniority, team spirit

Although America's geographic regions challenge the foreigner with different sets of ....[1] to operate within, no matter where you visit or attempt to do business in the USA, you will experience something that can be described as the 'American Way'.

The tempo of life in America is fast. Americans are generally busy and appear to be working at a rapid pace. Perhaps this is due to the credo 'time is money, and money talks'. Americans work hard, generally play hard, and employ all available technology and gadgets to increase their pace. Other people may work longer hours and seem to live for their work, such as the Japanese. Yet for the Japanese, patience, contemplation, and even silence are important virtues. Americans think in terms of hours and days and the all-important ....[2]. This tends to make ....[3] in the USA more ....[4] than in Japan, Europe, and the Australasian region.

The American attitude of ....[5] does not encourage socializing and getting to know business partners. Americans tend to have 'power breakfasts' and brief business lunches that are highly ....[6] to achieving business goals. People in other cultures will commit a lot of time and energy establishing relationships with business colleagues, whereas Americans tend to be more dedicated to ....[7].

Americans work by ....[8]. Given ....[9], they very often race to beat or achieve them. Giving deadlines elsewhere may produce alternative results, because of cultural differences that do not recognize that giving a task a deadline increases its importance and creates a sense of urgency. Sometimes meeting the deadline is a more important ....[10] of performance than the job itself.

Americans tend to be direct, particularly in a business environment, and openly challenge ideas and issues. Assertive, they take initiatives and opportunities to speak about their problems. For people from other cultures, this can sometimes appear to be confrontational and seem offensive.

....................[11] in American business life are vital. However, these do not qualify in the same way as business relationships in some other cultures. Americans call this 'networking', where they are always prepared to sell something, whether it be a product, company, or themselves.

Meetings are a major source of ....[12], and workers rely on attending meetings to keep up with what's going on in the organization and industry.

The existence of ....[13] within US companies is often not visually pronounced. A CEO (chief executive officer) of a company often participates in day-to-day communication with employees of the company. Americans prefer to have their own offices where possible; ....[14] in the company is usually marked by a larger office or bigger window. In some areas, particularly in the high-technology industry, more traditional trappings of power (separate executive cafeterias or assigned parking spaces) have been purposely eliminated in an effort to show ....[15] across the organization.

6 Word stress

Mark the stress on the following words.

e.g. <u>cri</u>tical

1	cápital	11	matérial
2	clíent	12	nátional
3	cúltural	13	órient
4	cúrrent	14	pátent
5	devélopment	15	pérsonal
6	equípment	16	présent
7	evént	17	propósal
8	fináncial	18	sócial
9	glóbal	19	sùbstantial
10	góvernment	20	tálent

7 Spelling: UK vs USA

Some common American words have a different spelling from their British equivalents. Write the British equivalents next to the American spellings below.

1 aluminum ....

2 behavior ....

3 center ....

4 color ....

5 dialog ....

6 marvelous ....

7 modeled ....

8 practice (verb) ....

9 program ....

10 skeptical ....

11 sulfer ....

12 traveler ....

8 Cancelling an appointment

You have arranged to meet an important business client. This is her fax to you confirming the arrangements. Unfortunately something unexpected has cropped up. You cannot attend the meeting. Write an e-mail in apology to her, suggesting another time.

> It was good to hear from you the other day. I just wanted to confirm what we had arranged. You said you'll be arriving directly from the airport and should be here by around 9.00. I've arranged the meeting to start at 10.00, which should give us enough time to sort out any last minute details. In the evening I've planned a trip down the River Thames to Greenwich and we will be having dinner on the boat. Let me know if you need anything else arranging.
> Best regards
> Anna Southern

9 Tipping

Below are the typical tips (money to show satisfaction for a service) given in the USA for particular services. Fill in the third column. Then write a letter to a friend from the USA who is coming to visit your country. Make sure you give information about customs and habits in your country (e.g. tipping, public transport, checking into hotels, eating in restaurants, using the telephone).

Service	USA	Your country
hotel chambermaid	$1 per night or $5–$10 for longer stays	
hotel bellhop	$1 per bag; $0.50 for opening and showing you the room	
restaurant waiter / waitress	15% of bill	
taxi	15% of fare, no less than $0.25	
barber's / hairdresser's	15% of the cost, generally minimum of $1	
plane: in-flight personnel	none	

10 ENTERTAINING

1 Past tenses

Put the verbs in brackets into the past simple, the past continuous, or the past perfect.

A man and a woman ....¹ (have) dinner in a fine restaurant. Their waitress, who ....² (take) another order at a table a few paces away, ...³ (notice) that the man ....⁴ (slowly slide) down his chair and under the table with the woman acting unconcerned. The waitress ....⁵ (watch) as the man ....⁶ (slide) all the way down his chair and out of sight under the table. Still the woman who ....⁷ (dine) across from him ....⁸ (appear) calm and unruffled, apparently unaware that her dining companion ....⁹ (disappear). After the waitress ....¹⁰ (finish) taking the order, she ....¹¹ (come) over to the table and ....¹² (say) to the woman, 'Pardon me madam, but I think your husband just ....¹³ (slide) under the table.' The woman calmly ....¹⁴ (look) up at her and ....¹⁵ (reply) firmly: ' ... '

Now choose which you consider to be the right ending:

a 'No he didn't. He's just walked in the door.'
b 'He's a secret agent and doesn't want to be seen.'
c 'I know. He thinks he's a dog.'

2 Coffee break

It's time for a coffee break. Reorder the following sentences to form a dialogue between you and your guest. The dialogue begins in your office.

1 Black with no sugar. Do those croissants have anything inside? ☐

2 How do you like it? ☐

3 I'll have a coffee please. ☐

4 I'm not sure. I'll just ask. Yes, they have a little jam. Would you like one? ☐

5 It's just over there, through that door on the left. ☐

6 OK. But please let me pay for these. ☐

7 (your guest returns) Do you often come to this bar? ☐

8 That sounds like a good idea. Do you have a coffee machine? ☐

9 That's very kind of you, but this is on me. ☐

10 (you arrive at the café) What can I get you? ☐

11 This might be a good point to have a break. Shall we go and get a coffee? ☐

12 This one, or the one across the street. Well, I think we'd better get back to the meeting. ☐

13 Yes please. While they're bringing it I think I'll just go and freshen up. ☐

14 Yes we do, but we usually go to a café – there's one a couple of minutes away. ☐

3 Useful phrases: suggesting, offering, and recommending

Match the phrases in the first column with the answers in the second.

1 Fancy watching a match on Saturday?
2 Can I give you a hand with that?
3 The seats near the front are the best.
4 Would it be OK if we left a bit later?
5 Next time it'll be on me.

a By all means.
b I'll look forward to that.
c Sounds like a great idea.
d Thanks, but I think I can manage.
e Thanks, I'll try and get there early then.

4 Pronunciation: rhyming pairs?

Which of the following pairs of words don't rhyme? If the word has two syllables or more, only the last syllable has to rhyme.

bacon / taken
biscuit / transit
buffet / soufflé
cake / ache
champagne / campaign
cook / book
cuisine / fourteen

diet / quiet
food / good
fruit / boot
ham / lamb
mayonnaise / nowadays
meat / great
pea / three

pork / walk
recipe / receipt
roll / role
sauce / course
steak / speak
taste / last
wine / sign

5 What do you say when ...?

Write down the words you would use to respond to the following situations.

1 Your host asks you if you would mind him / her smoking.

....

2 You think that something that you are about to eat may be culturally

unacceptable.

....

3 You spill red wine all over your host's shirt and trousers / skirt.

....

4 You are invited by your host (or host's wife / husband) to dance.

....

5 You've already had too much food and there's another course on the way.

....

6 Your host keeps insisting on filling up your wine – but you don't want any more.

....

7 Your guest offers to pay the bill.

....

6 Letter-writing

Do one of the following tasks:

1 Write a reply to the following e-mail (from a friend on the opposite side of the globe).

> I have been invited by a big corporation in your town to deliver a presentation on my company's services. After the presentation we will be going out for dinner. As you know I've never visited your country before and the problem is I have no idea of the dinner table etiquette in your part of the world. Can you fill me in with a few do's and don'ts? Thanks very much. I'll give you a ring as soon as I arrive and maybe we could go out for a drink. Love to your family.

2 Write a thank-you letter to someone who gave you dinner at their house.

7 Table manners

1 Where would you take a foreign guest for dinner?

  a A typical restaurant which serves local specialities.

  b A restaurant run by people of your guest's nationality.

  c A high-class hotel serving international cuisine.

2 Which of the following would you not do at a restaurant?

  a Smoke.

  b Use a toothpick.

  c Only use a fork when a knife is available as well.

  d Make a phone call from the table on your mobile phone.

3 You've been given something to eat which you do not like the look of. What would you do?

  a Politely refuse to eat it.

  b Eat a part of it, then leave the rest on your plate.

  c When no one's looking remove the food from your plate and somehow make it disappear.

  d Pretend it's something else and eat all of it.

4 The bill comes and you realize you've left your credit card at home. What would you do?

  a Make a hasty telephone call to your husband / wife.

  b Have a quiet word with the restaurant owner.

  c Explain your predicament to your guest and ask him / her to pay; you're all on expenses, after all.

11 PRESENTATIONS

1 Advice on presentations

Here is some advice for presenters. Put a cross against any of the advice you don't agree with and briefly explain why.

Preparation

...... Arrive one hour early.

...... Meet, touch, and talk to the attendees before the presentation begins.

...... Memorize the first two minutes.

...... Use cheat sheets to write down the first three to five words you will say for each key item.

...... Have something showing on the screen when they walk in – the title page of your presentation.

Opening

In the first 120 seconds you must:

...... • capture their attention and interest

...... • answer the question 'What's in it for me?'

Tailor to the audience

...... Convey the perception that your presentation was created just for them.

Eye contact

...... We speak to people through our eyes. Don't handicap yourself. Look at the audience. More specifically, look directly at one person in the audience for three to five seconds.

Voice

...... The antidote for the monotone is a mix of conviction, enthusiasm, confidence, desire, and rehearsal.

Analogies

...... The world's best communicators use analogies to create easy-to-understand images of their key points or concepts.

The close

...... The most important part of the presentation is the close. They will remember best what they hear last. You should write out the last two minutes of the presentation and memorize it.

Questions and answers

...... Don't ask 'Are there any questions?' – you're likely to get dead silence.
A better way would be to ask: 'Are there any questions about the twelve techniques for ...'

...... If you don't know the answer or aren't sure – don't bluff.

2 Families

Write the opposite-sex equivalents of these words.

1 aunt ....
2 niece ....
3 husband ....
4 grandson ....
5 bachelor ....

3 Phrasal / prepositional verbs

Match the part in *italics* with a phrasal / prepositional verb from the box. Then replace the object with a pronoun and put it in the correct position.

> **1–5:** hand out, set out, sort out, turn out, work out
>
> **6–10:** check out, cut down, look after, set up, take over

1 I will now *distribute* some more information sheets.
   I will now hand them out.....................

2 They are *producing* cars at the rate of 5,000 a day.

   ....

3 They will try and *resolve* the problem.

   ....

4 They *explained* the details in this document.

   ....

5 We can't *understand* the small print.

   ....

6 They have (forcefully) *merged with* our company.

   ....

7 We would like to *be responsible for* the sales side.

   ....

8 We are going to have to *reduce* our sales force.

   ....

9 They have already *formed* the new company.

   ....

10 We will *investigate* the issue further.

   ....

4 Matching

Form a new noun or verb by matching a word on the left with one on the right. Then match the new words with the definitions (1–10) below.

buy	head	mark	under
ware	back	brain	brand
over	spin		

house	hunt	out	cut
up	date	heads	off
leader	storm		

1 set price for product at lower than competition's price ....

2 building where merchandise is stored ....

3 amount added to cost by retailer to set price for customer ....

4 purchase of company typically with borrowed money by management ....

5 search for personnel ....

6 new company created out of another company ....

7 total direct expenses in running a company ....

8 product with largest share of the market for all products of that type ....

9 collective idea-generation ....

10 set a date before the scheduled date ....

5 Word stress

Which of these words have the stress on the first syllable? If the stress changes depending on whether it is a noun or verb (e.g. *record*), assume it is a verb.

1	concept	11	exchange	21	income
2	concise	12	exclude	22	index
3	conclude	13	expand	23	inform
4	confirm	14	expert	24	input
5	connect	15	explain	25	instant
6	constant	16	export	26	invest
7	consult	17	express	27	invoice
8	contain	18	extend	28	increase
9	contents	19	extra	29	incur
10	control	20	extract	30	inspect

6 Arranging a presentation

You have been asked by a foreign company to give a presentation on your product / service at their premises. Write a brief letter thanking them for the invitation, and explaining:

– what equipment you will need
– how you would like the room to be laid out
– how long you think the presentation will take
– anything else you think is relevant.

They have asked you to give the presentation on the morning of the 14th of next month. This would not be convenient for you, so suggest another time, and let them know what time you would prefer to arrive.

7 Are you stressed out?

Answer *yes* or *no* to the following questions. Decide which *yes* answers are likely to cause stress.

		Yes	No
1	Are you very competitive?	☐	☐
2	Do you often take work home with you or study for long hours at a time?	☐	☐
3	Do you have to travel a lot for work or study?	☐	☐
4	Do you get very nervous before examinations (both academic and medical)?	☐	☐
5	Are you always in a rush?	☐	☐
6	Are you a good listener?	☐	☐
7	Do you often get angry with the stupidities of other drivers?	☐	☐
8	Are you worried about what people think of you?	☐	☐
9	Are you patient when waiting in queues?	☐	☐
10	Do you normally show your feelings?	☐	☐

Now look at the key on page 77 to find out how stressed you are!

8 Reading and punctuation

One of the most popular ways of closing a presentation is with an authoritative quotation. Here is a very famous one written by John Ruskin. First punctuate it. Then practise reading it aloud.

> its unwise to pay too much but its worse to pay too little when you pay too much you lose a little money thats all when you pay too little you sometimes lose everything because the thing you bought was incapable of doing the thing it was bought to do the common law of business balance prohibits paying a little and getting a lot it cant be done if you deal with the lowest bidder it is well to add something for the risk you run and if you do that you will have enough to pay for something better

9 Target words

Some presenters believe that certain words are particularly useful for 'hitting your target' by instilling messages into people's heads during presentations. Here are some of those words. Begin in the middle of the target and work round either clockwise or anticlockwise, e.g. love:

Are there any of these words that you would never consider using in a presentation?

12 PERFORMANCE

1 Test your performance

1 Match the instructions with the figures below, then carry out the tasks. Spend no more than thirty seconds on each task.

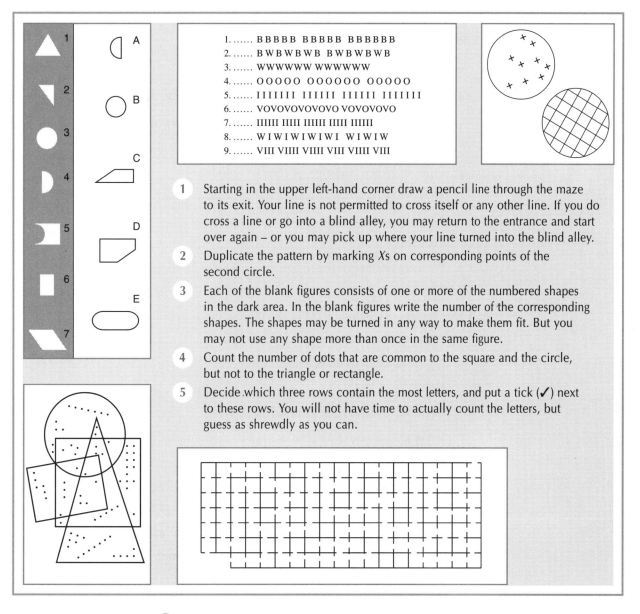

1. ...... BBBBB BBBBB BBBBBB
2. ...... BWBWBWB BWBWBWB
3. ...... WWWWWW WWWWWW
4. ...... OOOOO OOOOOO OOOOO
5. ...... IIIIIII IIIIII IIIIII IIIIIII
6. ...... VOVOVOVOVOVO VOVOVOVO
7. ...... IIIIII IIIII IIIII IIIII IIIII
8. ...... WIWIWIWIWI WIWIW
9. ...... VIII VIIII VIIII VIII VIIII VIII

1 Starting in the upper left-hand corner draw a pencil line through the maze to its exit. Your line is not permitted to cross itself or any other line. If you do cross a line or go into a blind alley, you may return to the entrance and start over again – or you may pick up where your line turned into the blind alley.

2 Duplicate the pattern by marking *X*s on corresponding points of the second circle.

3 Each of the blank figures consists of one or more of the numbered shapes in the dark area. In the blank figures write the number of the corresponding shapes. The shapes may be turned in any way to make them fit. But you may not use any shape more than once in the same figure.

4 Count the number of dots that are common to the square and the circle, but not to the triangle or rectangle.

5 Decide which three rows contain the most letters, and put a tick (✔) next to these rows. You will not have time to actually count the letters, but guess as shrewdly as you can.

2 Now match the instructions with these short explanations of what they are supposed to test. Do you agree?

a Demonstrates potential skill in a wide variety of tasks. These range from wrapping and packing to making the spatial adjustments required in handling tools and assembling.

b Checks ability to devote to a task the care and thoroughness it properly deserves.

c Verifies capacity to make quick decisions.

d Inventiveness can be regarded as a matter of combining existing forms into new ones, of taking elements of old patterns and synthesizing them into new patterns. This task tests such a creative ability.

e Measures anticipation and the ability to foresee, along with speed of learning.

2 Job description

Choose a project that you are working on at the moment (or have worked on in the past). Imagine that you require a new person to join your project team. Write a brief job description including any of the five skills from exercise 1 that you think are needed to do the job. First describe the kind of work involved, and then the type of person you are looking for.

3 Permission and obligation

Finish the second sentence so that it means the same as the first.

1 This program allows revisions to be made directly on the screen.

   This program lets ....

2 Don't mix them together or they'll explode.

   They must ....

3 They let us come to work when we want.

   They don't make ....

4 We were not permitted to smoke during the meeting.

   They didn't allow ....

5 Changes can be made while assembling the system.

   The system allows changes ....

6 Are we obliged to do it straight away?

   Do we ....

7 It wasn't necessary for us to arrive so early.

   We didn't ....

8 We were forced to leave our car at the border.

   We had ....

9 It would have been better if you had come yesterday.

   You ....

10 It isn't necessary to do it immediately, you can do it later.

   You ....

4 Complaining

Write a letter of complaint about the non-arrival of some parts you ordered. Improvise as much as you like around the information below.

• Today's date:	15 April
• Date parts were ordered:	10 March
• Agreed delivery date:	20 March
• Previous communications re this matter:	21 March, 1 April
• Result of non-arrival of parts:	delay in delivery of machines to several customers

5 Word stress

Below are some verbs with their corresponding nouns. Underline the stressed syllables, and mark them according to whether they have the stress on the same (*S*) syllable or a different (*D*) syllable.

e.g. <u>au</u>dit, <u>au</u>ditor _____*S*_____

coin<u>cide</u>, co<u>in</u>cidence _____*D*_____

1 acknowledge / acknowledgement ....
2 advertise / advertisement ....
3 appraise / appraisal ....
4 appreciate / appreciation ....
5 authorize / authority ....
6 cancel / cancellation ....
7 compare / comparable ....
8 deduct / deduction ....
9 economic / economical ....
10 enhance / enhancement ....

11 enclose / enclosure ....
12 exhibit / exhibition ....
13 expect / expectancy ....
14 insure / insurance ....
15 perform / performance ....
16 proceed / procedure ....
17 promote / promotion ....
18 settle / settlement ....
19 specify / specification ....
20 substitute / substitution ....

6 Job application

① Write brief notes in the table below. Think about what you have already achieved, and what progress you still have to make. You don't have to tell the truth!

Personal Assessment Sheet

	now	1/5/10 years ago (you choose)
position		
qualifications		
technical expertise		
communication skills		
managerial skills		
level of English		
job satisfaction		
vision of future		

② Imagine you have applied for a new job. You have been asked to write a brief resume in connected speech about your career history. Use the information you have written in the table as a basis for your resume.

7 Company performance

Insert the words below into the correct spaces.

> **1–6**: manufacturer, margins, performance, productivity, profit, tax
>
> **7–12**: break-even, competitors, growth, market, restructuring, sales

Restructured Whirlpool advances 58%

By Nikki Tait in Chicago

Better results from its European operations and a strong _____ [1] in its core North American market helped Whirlpool, the biggest _____ [2] of large home appliances in the USA, to post a 58 per cent recovery in first-quarter _____ [3] from continuing operations, at $68m after _____ [4].

The company said yesterday there had been continued _____ [5] improvements in its North American business, leading to higher _____ [6] and record profit levels.

Europe – which has been a problematic _____ [7] for both Whirlpool and some of its large _____ [8] in recent years – also benefited from better product shipments and cost-reduction moves.

The group said it believed there would be continued performance improvements in the region. Again, it lifted its forecast for industry _____ [9] to about 3 per cent, up from previous estimates of about 2 per cent.

Latin America was less encouraging, with _____ [10] declining on the back of weaker conditions in the big Brazilian market, although Whirlpool said performance had been 'solid'.

Meanwhile, the Asian business was 'at planned levels' with _____ [11] efforts said to be on schedule. The company reaffirmed its target of reaching _____ [12] – or close to this – for the full year.

13 NEGOTIATING

1 Negotiating over the phone

Your company is interested in replacing its computers and has received a quote from a supplier. You are now phoning the supplier (B) to discuss their quote. Fill in the spaces with words and phrases from the box.

> **1–5**: in mind, margin, peripherals, quote, target price
>
> **6–11**: at no extra charge, brief, concessions, go so far, include, states
>
> **12–17**: a deal, agreed, bear in mind, overall costs, run through, substantial

A I got your ....[1] this morning. You've come very close to our ....[2] for the computers themselves.

B Good.

A However, I think we need to take a closer look at some of the ....[3].

B I see. Perhaps you could tell me more exactly what you mean.

A Well, I'd say there are several areas. Let's take them one at a time. Printers, for example. Your price is much higher than we had ....[4].

B There's actually not much of a ....[5] on printers, and we can only really ....[6] on that.

A Well, could you perhaps make us a few ....[7] on the training part?

B What did you have in mind?

A Well, your quote ....[8] a three-day training period for the new word processing package and spreadsheets.

B That's right.

A Perhaps that could be extended to ....[9] an extra two days for work on graphics. Would you be able to do that ....[10]?

B You didn't actually mention that in your ....[11], or did you?

A No, I'm sorry I didn't – it only occurred to me this morning. But I wouldn't have thought that would add much to your ....[12].

B Well it is actually quite a ....[13] cost to us.

A What about if those two days extra were at your offices rather than ours?

B Yes, well that would make a difference.

A So is that ....[14] then?

B I think I'd need to check with Mr Patel on that one first.

A Well, ...[15] that we're opening another office in the area very soon, so we could be putting quite a bit of business your way. And we are considering other quotations.

B OK, that sounds fine – two days extra training at our premises.

A Great! Well on that basis I think we've got ....[16]. So let me just ....[17] what we've decided – the hardware ...

2 Setting conditions

Complete the second sentence so that it means the same as the first.

1 If you let me know in advance, I'll get it all ready for you.

Provided ....

2 Lower the price or the deal is off.

Unless ....

3 Unless you need it immediately, I'd rather you took it next week.

If ....

4 We will increase your credit from 30 to 60 days on the condition that you extend the warranty.

If ....

5 Assuming that I can discuss it with her, I'll let you know by the end of today.

Unless ....

3 Stress and pronunciation

1 Which of the following words have the stress on the first syllable? If the word can be both a noun and a verb, assume it is a noun.

debate	define	discount	dispatch
debit	delay	discuss	dispute
decrease	delete	disease	dissolve
deduct	demand	diskette	distant
defect	detail	dismiss	distinct

2 In which cases is *de-* not pronounced /dɪ/? In which cases is *dis-* not pronounced /dɪs/?

4 Negotiating jargon

Match a phrase on the left with its meaning on the right.

1 bring price up / down   a accept
2 clinch a deal   b agree to give / allow something
3 last minute hitch   c bargaining area
4 make a concession   d conclude negotiations definitively
5 margin   e desired price
6 negotiating ground   f difference between buy / sell price
7 quotation   g final limit / offer
8 settle for   h raise or cut price
9 target price   i unexpected difficulty towards end
10 the bottom line   j statement of how much goods / services will cost

5 A follow-up

You have negotiated the installation of some equipment in your factory by JCN, an engineering company. Below are some notes that you took during the negotiation with Mr Lee of JCN. Question marks indicate points which were not resolved. Write a letter to Mr Lee expressing how you feel the negotiation went, and summarizing the main points.

	what was originally wanted	what was agreed
Price	$1,500,000	$1,800,000
Payment	90 days of receipt of invoice	90 days of receipt of invoice
Warranty	5 year	3 or 5 years?????
Installation costs	JCN to pay	JCN to pay
Maintenance costs	JCN to pay	to be borne by us
Delivery costs	JCN to pay	JCN to pay if we pay import duties
Contract to be drawn up	end of this month	end of this/next month????
Next meeting	????	????

6 Test your negotiating power

The following different opinions about negotiating style appear in *Negotiate to Close* by management consultant Gary Karrass. Decide whether they are true or false, and if false, explain briefly why. Check your answers with the key on page 79.

1 We should always give reasons for our proposal, why the price is what it is. Buyers like and need explanations with proposals. They like explanations themselves and they are able to pass on the explanations to their bosses. ....

2 Those who think they have no power negotiate poorly and weakly – even if they do have power. Those who think they have power negotiate from strength – even if they don't really have the power. ....

3 The seller who gets the highest price is always the happiest seller. Right? The buyer who gets the lowest price is always the happiest buyer. Right? ....

4 The buyer will object to the price whether he has a price objection or not. That's what he's supposed to do. He will try and get the price down even if he doesn't think it's too high. ....

5 At Harvard Graduate School of Business Administration researchers put up a partition in the middle of a small room. Hundreds of people negotiated, two at a time – one coming in one door, the other coming in the other door. Half the negotiators were told the typical bargainer in their position got $7.50. The other half were told $2.50. What did they average? $5. ....

6 When the buyer says he will only spend a certain amount, it's true, at the moment he says it. A few minutes later his mind may change. That amount may change. In negotiation, truth shifts, moves around. What is true at one moment may disappear and within minutes there is a different truth. It doesn't mean the first truth wasn't valid. ....

7 The buyer knows exactly what he wants and needs no help in making his decision. ....

8 The buyer wants to be listened to. The more you listen to the buyer's wants, needs, and problems, the better he will like it. And the more you will learn about him and his organization. ....

9 Make the contract or agreements as detailed as possible, to cover demand or request situations that may possibly arise in the future. The more detailed the agreement, the less chance of misunderstanding. ....

14 TRADE

1 Letter-writing

1 An exhibitor sends a visitor the following quotation. Correct any mistakes you find, including those related to layout.

Meta 4 PLC

Downing Street, 10

Manchester

M16 ONZ

Manchester, december 2th 2107

Dear Ms Green,

        Subject: request for quotation

further to Your letter of 10 / 11 / 07 we have got pleasure in enclosing a quotation for the items following:

FaseOut 2110	$10m
FaseOut Turbo Expander	$100,000

Please, do not hesitate to contact us you should need any further informations. We are looking forward to hear from You in the next future.

        sincerely Yours

        Engineer A. Moronovic

2 Now write a reply, accepting the quotation and placing an order for two FaseOut 2110s and one Turbo Expander.

2 Complaints and mistakes

Below are some extracts from letters addressed to you. Write brief and suitable replies to three of the following extracts from letters, improvising and inventing as you wish. Choose the letters that seem most relevant to your company's needs.

1 Seeing as you are now one month behind schedule with your deliveries, we think a further 5% discount on outstanding deliveries would be a suitable compensation to offset all the difficulties we have had to incur.

2 We would be grateful if you could inform us whether the new licence agreement still includes the 18-month maintenance terms. Could you also let us know if you are planning to release an updated version which is compatible with DROW 8.0?

3 We are still awaiting delivery of lot #434, despite having received advice of shipment from you more than two weeks ago.

4 There appears to be some mistake in your last invoice No. 254 dated 28 November, as the VAT does not tally with the total amount due. I would be grateful if you could look into this and let us know as soon as possible, as we will shortly be closing our books for this year.

5 We would also like to take this opportunity to clarify a few questions in relation to your recent quotation. Would your agent here be able to offer the same service terms as outlined in your original quotation? Could deliveries be made twice monthly, rather than monthly? Finally, could all the manuals be translated into English (at no extra charge to us)?

6 On checking our credit card statement we discovered that we have inadvertently been charged for twenty items, whereas the shipment form clearly states that we ordered and received ten items.

7 Although the number of packages is correct, of the ten we have opened so far, nine have parts missing (specifically, parts #787, #791, and #803). As this is not the first time this has happened we would be grateful for immediate action.

3 Spot the odd word out

Find the odd word out in each group of words. Then give a reason why.

1   stand, hall, floor space, badge ....
2   brochure, catalogue, leaflet, menu ....
3   attendee, guest, salesman, visitor ....
4   retailer, supplier, sponsor, wholesaler ....
5   manufacturer, buyer, distributor, host ....
6   jammed, damaged, faulty, imperfect ....
7   overdraft, debt, deficit, surplus ....
8   careless, inefficient, unreliable, inadequate ....
9   seminar, conference, infrastructure, workshop ....
10 versatile, substandard, effective, flexible ....

4 Pronunciation

Put a cross in the box for the pairs that are not pronounced in exactly the same way.

1   cents / sense ☐
2   fare / fair ☐
3   our / hour ☐
4   guessed / guest ☐
5   hire / higher ☐
6   hole / whole ☐
7   mail / male ☐
8   tough / though ☐
9   sale / sail ☐
10 sum / some ☐
11 threw / through ☐
12 wait / weight ☐

5 Foreign words

Via international trade, the English language has adopted a lot of foreign words. Can you match these words with their language of origin?

1 caravan	6 igloo	11 restaurant	16 vodka
2 clan	7 kangaroo	12 robot	17 yacht
3 coffee	8 kindergarten	13 saga	18 yak
4 curry	9 maize	14 sauna	19 zebra
5 goulash	10 piano	15 tea	20 zero

a Native Australian	f Gaelic (Scottish or Irish)	k Turkish	p Dutch
b Eskimo	g Tamil (India)	l Cuban Spanish	q Chinese
c Hungarian	h Czech	m Icelandic	r Russian
d Persian	i Finnish	n Italian	s Arabic
e Tibetan	j French	o Congolese	t German

6 Reporting problems

Read the report form. Would you find it useful? If so, why?

Computer problem report form

1 Describe your problem:

....

....

2 Now, describe the problem accurately:

....

....

3 Speculate wildly about the cause of the problem:

....

....

4 Problem severity:

a Minor .... b Minor .... c Minor .... d Trivial ....

5 Is it turned on?

Yes .... No ....

6 Have you tried to fix it yourself?

Yes .... No ....

7 Have you made it worse?

Yes ....

8 What were you doing with your computer at the time the problem occurred?

....

9 If you answered 'nothing' then explain why you were logged in?

....

10 Are you sure you aren't imagining the problem?

Yes .... No ....

11 Is there anyone else you could blame this problem on?

Yes .... No ....

12 Have you given the machine a good whack on the top?

Yes .... No ....

13 Is the machine on fire?

Yes .... Not yet ....

14 Can you do something else instead of bothering me?

Yes .... No ....

7 Anagrams

Create a new word by using all the letters of the first word, e.g. *design > signed*. The first and last letters have been done for you. The clues will help you!

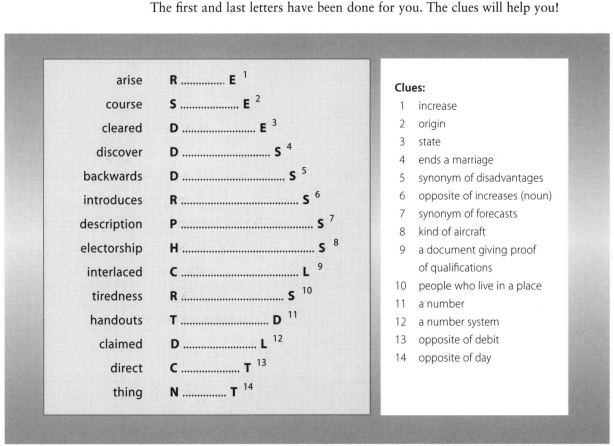

arise	R .... E	1	
course	S .... E	2	
cleared	D .... E	3	
discover	D .... S	4	
backwards	D .... S	5	
introduces	R .... S	6	
description	P .... S	7	
electorship	H .... S	8	
interlaced	C L	9	
tiredness	R .... S	10	
handouts	T .... D	11	
claimed	D L	12	
direct	C .... T	13	
thing	N .... T	14	

Clues:

1 increase
2 origin
3 state
4 ends a marriage
5 synonym of disadvantages
6 opposite of increases (noun)
7 synonym of forecasts
8 kind of aircraft
9 a document giving proof of qualifications
10 people who live in a place
11 a number
12 a number system
13 opposite of debit
14 opposite of day

8 *do* and *make*

Underline the correct form.

1 What have you been *doing / making*? We've been waiting for over an hour.
2 I'm sorry but if you wish to continue *doing / making* business with us you'll have to *do / make* better than this.
3 We have been invoiced twice for the same order. You must have *done / made* a mistake.
4 The delivery was supposed to have been *done / made* yesterday not today.
5 We couldn't have *done / made* the tests last week because we didn't have the samples then.
6 I'm sorry I haven't got the invoice ready yet. I promise I'll get it *done / made* by this evening.
7 You *did / made* us one offer at the trade fair, and now you appear to be *doing / making* a completely different proposal.
8 We have been *doing / making* watches for over 100 years now, and we've never *done / made* such a profit as this year.

Answer key

1 PROTOCOL

1 Introductions

Possible replies and alternatives (from formal to informal):

1 Very well thank you. / Fine thanks. / Not bad.
2 Good to see you too. / You too.
3 Pleased to meet you. / Hi, how are you doing?
4 How do you do? I'm ... / Hi, I'm ...
5 Oh, thank you. / Really? Good things I hope! / It's all lies!
6 Yes it is considering the time of year. / Yes, great! / Better than in England I bet!
7 It's ... . And yours is ... , right?
8 It's been a pleasure for me too. / Yes, you too – we mustn't leave it so long before the next time.
9 Yes of course. / I'll do that.
10 Yes, I'll look forward to that. / Great, see you then.

2 Question forms

1 Are you thinking
2 you have ever had
3 Did you have
4 Did you have; did you feel
5 Have you ever been convicted
6 do you drink
7 do / would you consider; do you do
8 do you generally do
9 do you see
10 does 'success' mean

4 The English

1	C	5	A
2	C	6	A
3	B	7	B
4	A		

5 Test your protocol

1 F (both hands)
2 T
3 F (Tau is her surname)
4 all T (in France this may vary from region to region)
5 T
6 T
7 F
8 F (it's part of Great Britain and the United Kingdom)
9 F (in some countries this sign is offensive)
10 F (in some cultures this is regarded as aggressive)

6 Answering the phone

Possible answers:

1 Hold the line please, I'll just check if he / she's here.
2 So, that's Donald Biggs – B-I-G-G-S?
3 Who shall I say is calling? / Could I have your name please?
4 Sorry to keep you waiting.
5 Sorry, I didn't quite catch that.
6 Sorry, could you speak a bit more slowly please?
7 Sorry, the line is bad. Could you speak up a bit please?
8 I'm sorry but he / she's in a meeting. Can I take a message or shall I get him / her to ring you back?
9 So that's 0161–928–007. / Could I just read that back to you – 01 ...
10 Thank you very much. Goodbye.

7 Telephone dialogues

1 This is
2 Could I speak to
3 I'm afraid
4 isn't here
5 could you ask him to call
6 me back
7 spell your name, please?
8 That's right.
9 Could you repeat that, please?
10 That's right
11 I'll give Mr Rossi your message.

2 MEETINGS

2 The ideal meeting?

1 b
2 f
3 a
4 c
5 d
6 e

This is obviously a humorous piece and if you followed the advice your meeting would be far from ideal!

3 Word stress

Words with different stress patterns:

First column: effective 2, agenda 1, objective 2, proceedings 2

Second column: calculate 1, character 1, database 1, management 1

Third column: organize 1, consumer 2, committee 2, register 1, revenue 1

4 Useful phrases: politics

1 bandwagon
2 old guard
3 swing vote
4 smear campaign
5 dark horse
6 landslide
7 fund raiser
8 grass roots
9 exit poll

5 More political terms

Across:

1 cabinet
6 minister
11 Secretary
13 reshuffle
14 aid
15 election

Down:

2 ban
3 Treasury
4 Commons
5 constituency
6 MP
7 scandals
8 Home
9 benefit
10 act
12 bill
13 riot

3 ORGANIZATION

1 Organizational culture

1 overriding
2 band
3 benefit
4 firms
5 generated
6 welfare
7 format
8 standpoint
9 dovetailed
10 markets

The text refers to Model 2 (known as The Mass).

3 Useful phrases

1

1 e: retail trade
2 a: strategic objective
3 d: corporate strategy
4 b: middle manager
5 c: information sharing
6 g: workforce
7 h: networking
8 j: turnover
9 f: backdate
10 i: warehouse

2

1	e	6	g
2	a	7	f
3	b	8	h
4	c	9	j
5	d	10	i

4 Do you have executive potential?

1 a
2 b
3 a
4 b

Score 3 points for each correct answer. Subtract 2 points each time you answered 'c'.

10–12   You will soon reach an executive level if you aren't already there.

8–9   You have executive potential, but still a little to learn.

6–7   Your capacity to handle people is limited.

0–5   Life for you must be extremely difficult!

5 job vs work

1 work; have made / have been making
2 She has finally reached; job
3 Did you do; I just did; jobs
4 have you been doing; you have not done; work
5 You have been doing; I have already finished; work

6 Pronunciation

1

/ɜː/   her, sir

/ɔː/   core, law, pour, raw

/eə/   fare, pair, square, they're

/eɪ/   play, they

2

Z   2, 3, 5, 7, 8, 9, 10, 12, 13, 14, 15, 18, 19, 20
S   1, 4, 6, 11, 16, 17

7 Education word search

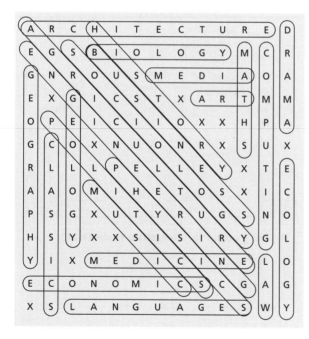

4 NUMBERS

1 The story of numbers

1 d
2 a
3 b
4 c
5 g
6 f
7 e

2 Prepositions

1 of
2 –; in
3 from; to
4 in
5 –
6 at; as
7 in
8 to

3 one vs a / an

1 a
2 one
3 one
4 a
5 a / one
6 one
7 a
8 one
9 a / one; once
10 a

4 Countable or uncountable?

The following can be countable:

coffee: when ordering in a café, 'two coffees please' is more usual than 'two cups of coffee'. Also tea, beer, mineral water.

hair: one individual hair

interest: a hobby

knowledge: of a specific thing, e.g. a knowledge of wine

paper: a thesis or essay on a given subject

work: a specific piece of work, such as a work of art, a work of fiction

5 Singular or plural?

1 is
2 is / are
3 is
4 are
5 doesn't
6 say
7 is
8 is
9 costs
10 is

6 Articles

1	the	18	–	35	the
2	a	19	a	36	the
3	a	20	–	37	– / the
4	an	21	the	38	–
5	a	22	–	39	–
6	the	23	the	40	a
7	a	24	a	41	a
8	–	25	–	42	the
9	a	26	the	43	a
10	a	27	the	44	a
11	the	28	an	45	a
12	the	29	–	46	a
13	–	30	the	47	the
14	a	31	the	48	the
15	the	32	–	49	the / an
16	a	33	the	50	a / the / –
17	the	34	a		

7 Money word search

8 Word stress

1 assets, budget, business, colleague, complex, concept, contents, credit, current, defect, factor, foreign, forecast, income, logo, outlet, product, profit, survey (n)

2 command, consist, control, correct, event, per cent, response, restrict, return, survey (vb), towards

9 Pronunciation

1 ✓ /e/ as in *yes*
2 /iː/ as in *feet*; /e/ as in *yes*
3 ✓ /aɪ/ as in *time*
4 /ɔː/ as in *four*; /aʊ/ as in *now*
5 /ʌ/ as in *fun*; /juː/ as in *new*
6 ✓ /ʌ/ as in *fun*
7 /ɔː/ as in *four*; /eə/ as in *fair*
8 ✓ /ʌ/ as in *fun*
9 /eɪ/ as in *eight*; /aɪ/ as in *time*
10 /ɪə/ as in *here*; /eə/ as in *fair*

10 Number games

1 The correct calculation should be that they have given £25 to the restaurant, plus £2 to the waiter, and kept a total of £3 for themselves. Another way of looking at it is to say that they have spent £9 each, making £27 (£25 + £2) plus the £3.

2   2 9 4

    7 5 3

    6 1 8

3 Three. The guard says a number and you merely tell him how many letters there are in that number.

4 $57 + 23 = 80 + 1 + 4 + 6 + 9 = 100$

11 Comparisons

1 earliest; around fourteen forty to fourteen hundred

2 smallest; a / one fiftieth

3 heaviest; ten point two kilos (twenty-two pounds, eight ounces); nineteen fifty-five

4 fastest; thirty-nine thousand, eight hundred (and) ninety-seven kilometers per / an hour

5 highest; one in two (but we say 'the ratio is one to two')

12 *arise, raise, rise*

1 has been rising / has risen
2 rose
3 raises
4 arose
5 are you going to raise / will you be raising / are you raising

5 COMMUNICATION

1 Telephone dialogue

Possible answers:

1 Sorry, I didn't catch your name.
2 I'm sorry but the line's engaged. Shall I get Mr Smith to call you back?
3 Sorry, what did you say?
4 I'm afraid the line's still engaged. Would you like to leave a message?
5 Has he got your number?
6 Can I read that back to you?
7 0171–980–4176
8 67 right. What time can Mr Smith call you?
9 OK, I'll make sure he gets your message Ms O'Reilly.

2 Useful phrases: letter writing

1 B
2 A
3 C
4 F
5 D
6 A
7 E
8 B, C
9 F
10 E

3 Indirect speech

1 He asked if he could speak to Mr Jones.
2 She said she was sorry but she hadn't quite caught what he (had) said.
3 He said he thought she must have dialled the wrong number.
4 He said (he was afraid) that she no longer worked there.
5 He asked her where she was calling from.
6 She asked him if he would like to hold the line or whether she should get Ms Smith to ring him back.
7 He said (he was afraid) that Ms Green had just left the office but that she should be back in half an hour.

8 She said that she would check for him.
9 He suggested spelling the word(s) for her. He asked if he should spell the word(s) for her.
10 She apologized for keeping him (waiting) and hoped that he hadn't been waiting long.

4 Linking words

1

a in addition to
b in fact
c despite
d whereas
e although
f likewise
g conversely
h apart from
i specifically
j alternatively

2

1 in connection with
2 Due to
3 also
4 Alternatively
5 However
6 as
7 Therefore
8 Finally

5 Keyboard

1	&	12	'
2	*	13	:
3	@	14	,
4	–	15	{ }
5	!	16	.
6	-	17	;
7	#	18	' ' " "
8	%	19	[ ]
9	( )	20	\
10	~	21	/
11	< >		

6 TRAVEL

2 Future trips

1 be seeing; ask; travel
2 see; trip
3 be going; journey
4 trip; have
5 arrive / be arriving; journey; take

4 Buying a rail ticket

Possible answers:

1 How much is a return / round trip to London?
2 I want to leave about 12 o'clock. / I'll be leaving about 1 o'clock.
3 Do I have to come back on a particular train? / How long is the ticket valid?
4 Can I pay by credit card? / Do you take American Express?
5 Do I have to change trains?
6 Which platform does it leave from?

5 What do you say when ...?

Possible answers:

1 Could I have a seat in non-smoking, please?
2 Excuse me, did you hear that announcement? / Sorry, but were they announcing flight no. ...?
3 Excuse me. I'm travelling on flight no. BA 127 but I (seem to) have lost my boarding card.
4 When you've finished reading that, would you mind if I took a look? / Could I possibly borrow that after you've finished reading it?
5 Could you possibly tell me how the phone works / how to use the phone, please?
6 Could you tell me where the car rental agencies are please?
7 (Roughly) how much will it cost me to get to the Hilton?
8 Here's something for your troubles. / Please keep the change.

6 Car parts

a 7
b 1
c 4
d 5
e 6
f 8
g 9
h 3
i 11
j 10
k 2
l 12

7 Travel vocabulary: USA vs UK

1 truck
2 overpass
3 subway
4 intersection
5 sidewalk
6 automobile
7 freeway
8 gasoline
9 pavement
10 return (ticket)

8 Opposites

1 departure
2 delayed / late
3 furthest / farthest
4 return / round trip
5 to land
6 get off
7 get out of
8 in front of
9 manual / shift-drive
10 taken

7 PLANNING

1 Rules of economics?

1 tradeoffs
2 give up
3 margin
4 incentives
5 trade
6 economic
7 outcomes
8 standard
9 rise
10 inflation

2 Silent letters

1 g: /rɪ'saɪn/
2 i: /'bɪznɪs/
3 s: /aɪl/
4 i: /su:t/
5 k: /nɒb/
6 k, w: /'nɒlɪdʒ/
7 l: /kɑ:m/
8 c: /'saɪəns/
9 u: /gærən'ti:/
10 b: /det/

3 Stress

1 applicant, application: D
2 attend attendee: D
3 available, availability: D
4 compete, competitive: D
5 economic, economical: S
6 efficient, efficiency: S
7 engine, engineer: D
8 feasible, feasibility: D
9 hypothesis, hypothetical: D
10 liable, liability: D
11 machine, machinery: S
12 method, methodology: D
13 production, productivity: D
14 profit, profitable: S
15 reliable, reliability: D
16 sequence, sequential: D
17 standard, standardize: D
18 strategy strategic: D
19 technique, technical: D
20 theory, theoretical: D

4 Future simple and future perfect

1 be
2 have worked
3 have reached
4 have achieved
5 get
6 stop; start
7 be

5 Environment word search

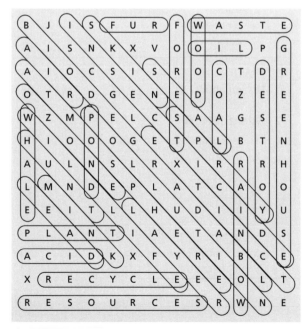

7 Business plans

8 PRODUCTS

2 Word stress

The stress is different in these groups:

6 employ   employee   employment
8 install   installer   installation
9 interpret   interpreter   interpretation
12 negotiate   negotiator   negotiation
13 organize   organizer   organization

3 Devices word search

4 The passive

1 Plans are being made for the future.
2 You have already been told twice.
3 It will be finished by the end of the day.
4 This must be done before 12.00.
5 He was seen leaving the building.

5 Useful phrases: general business

1	e	6	g
2	d	7	f
3	c	8	j
4	a	9	h
5	b	10	i

6 Test your mechanical aptitude

1 diagram
2 drives
3 drives
4 turns
5 arrow
6 cause
7 to move
8 as
9 to
10 as
11 counterclockwise
12 being
13 to turn
14 spring
15 therefore
16 since / because
17 since / because
18 because
19 follows
20 clockwise
21 then
22 so
23 to stop
24 or
25 causing
26 to move

Answers to quiz:

1 b
2 c

8 *Chindogu*

1 The *Chindogu* is a chin switch. It allows you to turn a light switch on and off with your chin if your hands are not clean.

9 VISITING

1 Pronunciation

/θ/ thank, theory, thesis, thing, threshold, authority, mathematics, method, cloth, length, path, strength, twelfth, health

/ð/ that, thus, algorithm, breathe, clothing, without, with

2 Asking about a flight

Possible answers:

1 Did you have a smooth flight?
2 Was the flight on time?
3 How long was the flight?
4 What was the food like?
5 Where are you staying?
6 What was the weather like when you left?

3 Countries

1 Sweden, Swedish, Swedish
2 Switzerland, Swiss, French / German / Italian
3 Turkey, Turkish, Turkish
4 Denmark, Danish, Danish
5 Austria, Austrian, German
6 Mexico, Mexican, Spanish
7 Egypt, Egyptian, Arabic
8 Poland, Polish, Polish
9 Thailand, Thai, Thai
10 Wales, Welsh, Welsh / English

4 What do you say when ...?

Possible answers (if you wish to avoid answering directly):

1 Thank you very much indeed, that's most kind. I'm afraid I haven't brought anything myself – I've come straight from the office / railway station.
2 Yes, you're probably right. / No, I can't say I agree with you.
3 To be honest I don't know – I haven't had it valued recently.
4 Not as much as I'd like to!
5 Do you mind if I smoke? I can go outside if you like.
6 I really am very sorry, you must let me replace it.
7 I'm very sorry, did I say something out of turn?
8 Shall we move on to dessert?

5 The 'American Way'

1 frameworks
2 fiscal quarter
3 goal structuring
4 short term
5 'let's get down to business'
6 geared
7 getting the job done
8 schedules
9 deadlines
10 measure
11 personal connections
12 information exchange
13 hierarchy
14 seniority
15 team spirit

6 Word stress

1 capital
2 client
3 cultural
4 current
5 development
6 equipment
7 event
8 financial
9 global
10 government
11 material
12 national
13 orient
14 patent
15 personal
16 present (n) present (vb)
17 proposal
18 social
19 substantial
20 talent

7 Spelling: UK vs USA

1 aluminium
2 behaviour
3 centre
4 colour
5 dialogue
6 marvellous
7 modelled
8 practise
9 programme
10 sceptical
11 sulphur
12 traveller

10 ENTERTAINING

1 Past tenses

1 were having
2 was taking
3 noticed
4 was slowly sliding
5 watched
6 slid
7 was dining
8 appeared
9 had disappeared
10 had finished
11 came
12 said
13 slid
14 looked
15 replied

The right ending is: 'No he didn't. He's just walked in the door'.

2 Coffee break

11, 8, 14, 10, 3, 2, 1, 4, 13, 5, 7, 12, 6, 9

3 Useful phrases: suggesting, offering, and recommending

1 c   2 d   3 e   4 a   5 b

4 Pronunciation: rhyming pairs?

The following do not rhyme:

food / good; meat / great; recipe / receipt; steak / speak; taste / last

5 What do you say when ...?

Possible answers:

1 Would you mind not smoking? I've got a terrible cough.
2 Can you tell me exactly what's in this? I'm worried that there might be something in it that I'm not able to eat.
3 I really am extremely sorry. How clumsy of me. Please let me pay to get it cleaned.
4 Thank you very much indeed. / I'm sorry but I'm a really hopeless dancer and I'd rather not if you don't mind.
5 I really don't think I could eat any more. I'm not really used to eating so much.
6 Listen, I really don't want any more to drink. In any case I've got to drive back to the hotel.
7 That's really very kind of you, but this is on me.

7 Table manners

1 a Many travellers to foreign parts like to try new dishes, so this would probably be the most suitable choice.

   b The least appropriate choice because the cuisine is likely to have been adapted to suit the tastes of the host nation.

   c If you are not sure then this would be the safest option.

2 a In the UK, restaurants often have designated areas where smoking is permitted. In the USA, it is becoming more common for smoking not to be allowed at all in public places.

   b Some restaurants provide toothpicks, but diners generally try to be discreet in their use, if they use them at all.

   c This is fairly common in the USA, but less usual in the UK, especially in more exclusive restaurants.

   d This would depend on how well you know the other diners and on how the user is sitting in relation to other diners, but in any case is usually considered rude.

3 a This would be considered rude, especially if you are being served a local delicacy.

   b A diplomatic compromise!

   c If you really think you can get away with it, this would avoid causing offence.

   d The best solution, if you can do it.

4 a All very well if it is possible, and if you intend to stay in the restaurant for a while!

   b This would work if you have a good relationship with the owner; or you could ask for an invoice to be sent to your office.

   c This would not be considered acceptable in the UK.

11 PRESENTATIONS

2 Families

1	uncle	4	granddaughter
2	nephew	5	spinster
3	wife		

3 Phrasal / prepositional verbs

2 They are turning them out.
3 They will try and sort it out.
4 They set them out.
5 We can't work it out.
6 They have taken it over.
7 We would like to look after it.
8 We are going to have to cut it down.
9 They have already set it up.
10 We will check it out.

4 Matching

1	undercut	6	spin-off
2	warehouse	7	overheads
3	markup	8	brand leader
4	buyout	9	brainstorm
5	headhunt	10	backdate

5 Word stress

The following verbs have the stress on the first syllable:

concept, constant, contents, expert, extra, income, index, input, instant, invoice

7 Are you stressed out?

Score:

If you answered yes to six or more of questions 1–5 and 7–8 and no to the others, you are leading a very stressful life and you should take active steps to reduce your stress burden. If you answered yes to three or four of these questions, you are rather too worried about time and perhaps too ambitious. If you answered yes to two of the questions, your level of stress indicates that you lead a normal relaxed life. If you answered no to the above questions and yes to 6 and 9, then you are so relaxed that you're boring – wake up and live!

8 Reading and punctuation

It's unwise to pay too much, but it's worse to pay too little. When you pay too much, you lose a little money – that's all. When you pay too little, you sometimes lose everything, because the thing you bought was incapable of doing the thing it was bought to do. The common law of business balance prohibits paying a little and getting a lot – it can't be done. If you deal with the lowest bidder, it is well to add something for the risk you run, and if you do that, you will have enough to pay for something better.

9 Target words

you, time, money, health, comfort, enjoyment, guarantees, opportunity

new, save, glory, unique, results, advanced, discovery, achievement

12 PERFORMANCE

1 Test your performance

1

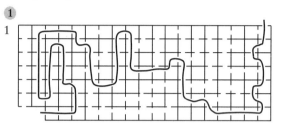

2

3 A 4; B 3; C 2+6; D 2+4+5+6 or 1+2+4+5;
   E 3+4+5
4 5
5 rows 5, 7, 9

2

1 e   2 a   3 d   4 b   5 c

3 Permission and obligation

1 This program lets you make revisions directly
   on the screen.
2 They must not be mixed together or they'll
   explode.
3 They don't make us come to work at a
   particular time.
4 They didn't allow us to smoke during the
   meeting.
5 The system allows changes to be made while
   assembling it.
6 Do we have to do it straight away?
7 We didn't need / have to arrive so early.
8 We had to leave our car at the border.
9 You should have come yesterday.
10 You don't have / need to do it immediately,
   you can do it later.

5 Word stress

1 acknowledge, acknowledgement: S
2 advertise, advertisement: D
3 appraise, appraisal: S
4 appreciate, appreciation: D
5 authorize, authority: D:
6 cancel, cancellation: D
7 compare, comparable: D
8 deduct, deduction: S
9 economic, economical: S

10 enhance, enhancement: S
11 enclose, enclosure: S
12 exhibit, exhibition: D
13 expect, expectancy: S
14 insure, insurance: S
15 perform, performance: S
16 proceed, procedure: S
17 promote, promotion: S
18 settle, settlement: S
19 specify, specification: D
20 substitute, substitution: D

7 Company performance

1 performance   7 market
2 manufacturer   8 competitors
3 profit   9 growth
4 tax   10 sales
5 productivity   11 restructuring
6 margins   12 break-even

13 NEGOTIATION

1 Negotiating over the phone

1 quote   10 at no extra charge
2 target price   11 brief
3 peripherals   12 overall costs
4 in mind   13 substantial
5 margin   14 agreed
6 go so far   15 bear in mind
7 concessions   16 a deal
8 states   17 run through
9 include

2 Setting conditions

Possible answers:

1 Provided you let me know …
2 Unless you lower the price, the deal is off.
3 If you don't need it immediately, I'd rather …
4 If you extend the warranty, we will increase …
5 Unless I can discuss it with her, I won't be able
   to let you know by the end of the day.

3 Stress and pronunciation

1 debit, decrease, defect, detail, discount, distant
2 debit, defect, detail (columns 1 and 2);
   disease, dissolve (columns 3 and 4)

4 Negotiating jargon

1	h	4	b	7	j	10	g
2	d	5	f	8	a		
3	i	6	c	9	e		

6 Test your negotiating power

All true (at least in America!), apart from:

3 It's much more important, in terms of satisfaction after a deal, how a price is reached than exactly what that price is. How the price is reached will affect any future relationships between the two parties.

5 The ones who aimed for $7.50 got about that, those who aimed for $2.50 got about that – the more you ask for, the more you get.

7 The opposite is often true. Many buyers deal with many products, many technologies. They cannot possibly keep up with them all.

14 TRADE

1 Letter-writing

1 General comments: It is now customary in the UK and USA to align all parts of the letter to the left, to use minimal punctuation in addresses, and to make dates as simple to read as possible. On a business letter, the sender's address will usually be in the form of a pre-printed letterhead, which could be anywhere at the top of the page but will always come before the receiver's address.

Suggested corrections:

```
Meta 4 PLC
10 Downing Street
Manchester
M16 0NZ

Receiver's address

2 December 2107

Re: request for quotation

Dear Ms Green

Further to your letter of 10 November
2107 we have pleasure in enclosing a
quotation for the following items:
FaseOut 2110                    $10m
FaseOut Turbo Expander          $100,000

Please do not hesitate to contact us
should you need any further information.
We look forward to hearing from you in
the near future.

Yours sincerely
Alexander Moronovic
```

3 Spot the odd word out

1 badge; the others all refer to areas of an exhibition centre
2 menu; the only one specifically about food
3 salesman; the only job
4 sponsor; the others are all sellers
5 host; the others are all involved in producing and selling goods
6 jammed; the only one which isn't damaged
7 surplus; the others refer to money which is owed
8 careless; can't be used for equipment, only people
9 infrastructure; the others are types of meetings
10 substandard; the rest are positive qualities

4 Pronunciation

1 and 8 are not pronounced in the same way.
Transcriptions are as follows:

1 /sents/, /sens/
2 /feə/
3 /aʊə/
4 /gest/
5 /haɪə/
6 /həʊl/
7 /meɪl/
8 /tʌf/, /ðəʊ/
9 /seɪl/
10 /sʌm/
11 /θruː/
12 /weɪt/

5 Foreign words

1	d	11	j
2	f	12	h
3	k	13	m
4	g	14	i
5	c	15	q
6	b	16	r
7	a	17	p
8	t	18	e
9	l	19	o
10	n	20	s

7 Anagrams

1 raise
2 source
3 declare
4 divorces
5 drawbacks
6 reductions
7 predictions
8 helicopters
9 credential
10 residents
11 thousand
12 decimal
13 credit
14 night

8 Do and make

1 doing
2 doing; do
3 made
4 made
5 done
6 done
7 made; making
8 making; made